Man Your Post

Man Your Post

Learning to Lead Like St. Joseph

Duane and Carrie Daunt

Foreword by Scott Hahn

TAN Books
Gastonia, North Carolina

Unless otherwise noted, Scripture quotations are from the Revised Standard Version of the Bible—Second Catholic Edition (Ignatius Edition), copyright © 2006 National Council of the Churches of Christ in the United States of America. Used by permission. All rights reserved.

Excerpts from the English translation of the *Catechism of the Catholic Church* for use in the United States of America © 1994, United States Catholic Conference, Inc.—Libreria Editrice Vaticana. Used with permission.

Cover design by Caroline Green

Cover image: Flight into Egypt (etching print) by Carlo Maratti. The Elisha Whittelsey Collection, The Elisha Whittelsey Fund, 1951, Metropolitan Museum of Art. Public domain via Wikimedia Commons.

Library of Congress Control Number: 2021940314

ISBN: 978-1-5051-2137-7
Kindle ISBN: 978-1-5051-2138-4
ePUB ISBN: 978-1-5051-2139-1

Published in the United States by
TAN Books
PO Box 269
Gastonia, NC 28053
www.TANBooks.com
Printed in the United States of America

Contents

Foreword

What's in a name? What's in a title?

In the case of St. Joseph, we can find an infinity of significance in the syllables by which we call him. A silent man, Joseph spoke volumes when he simply gave his name to the census taker in Bethlehem.

His name, after all, is a confession of hope. It means "God will increase." Joseph's lifetime was a strange interlude for God's Chosen People. Economically, they prospered. But they were ruled—illegitimately, according to the Law of Moses—by a murderous tyrant, Herod, who answered readily to the demands of his Gentile patrons, the Romans. He rebuilt the Jerusalem Temple, but he also subsidized the construction of idolatrous shrines in the Holy Land. Yet Joseph's name looked forward to the time of fulfillment, the day of the Messiah, which many believed to be imminent.

Joseph was known as a "son of David" (Mt 1:20). He was born into the royal clan from which the Messiah was expected to come. The family had been much diminished in the thousand years since David's reign. They had suffered exile and poverty. But they kept their sense of dignity and divine purpose. They safeguarded their identity in their genealogical tables, which historians tell us were carefully preserved even for centuries after the lifetime of Joseph. The clan of David remembered the marvels the Lord had done, and they knew that the arm of the Lord had not been short-ened in the intervening years. The name Son of David was still another expression of faith and hope.

Joseph's given name bespoke another foreshadowing in Israel's history. It evoked the memory of God's prodigies in the time of the patriarchs. The original Joseph was the most beloved son of Jacob and Rachel. And the father in the Holy Family had much in common with his ancient namesake. Both men brought their families to Egypt. Both received revelations in dreams. Both were righteous by any measure. By calling forth a new Joseph, God was fulfilling an implicit promise he had made almost two thousand years before. He was resolving an Old Testament type in a New Testament antitype.

Joseph's name spoke so eloquently that the saint, perhaps, did not need to say much. Saints and scholars make much of St. Joseph's silence. Scripture records not a single word from his mouth. It would be enough, however, for his people to know that he was *Joseph, Son of David*.

Everything after that is evidence of God's generosity—the superabundance of graces and glories that come to us with faith in Jesus Christ. As you'll see in the pages of this book, the treasury grows richer as the centuries pass and the Church deepens its reflection on the life of St. Joseph. We know him now as the Worker, Terror of Demons, and Patron of the Dying. We know him by names and titles implicit in his story, but drawn out only gradually, over millennia, through the development of Christian devotion and doctrine.

What emerges in this book is a powerful Catholic vision of manhood from a wide variety of Catholic men. And their witness points to the manly virtues of our common father figure. It's not the ideal we find in popular culture—where the ideal man moves through degrees of macho, from Rocky to Rambo. In Joseph, instead, we find a life that is silent so that God can speak. We find a man who reflects and prays before he acts. We find a man who cares more for his righteousness before God than his reputation before his neighbors. We find the antithesis of machismo, and yet we find the model of holy and courageous manhood.

This book is also an expression in words of the deeds of the John Paul II Healing Center, founded by Dr. Bob Schuchts, who is Carrie Daunt's father. I met Dr. Bob for the first time by phone, through a mutual friend, and I immediately got the sense that our initial conversation was itself a moment of grace, a sort of sacred serendipity—holy happenstance if you will.

Within minutes, it seems, we both figured out that we share a common background. Was it our accents? I wasn't sure.

"Wait," he said, "are you from Pittsburgh?"

"Well, yes. Yes, I am."

"What part?"

"The South Hills."

"Which town?"

"Bethel Park."

"What neighborhood?"

"Oakhurst."

"Where in Oakhurst?"

"Marshall Road."

"Marshall Road! What was your address?"

"Three-nineteen."

"Three-nineteen? That's just a few doors up the street from where I lived! Wait, did you have a brother named Fritz?"

It turns out that he grew up on the same block as the Hahn family, and our brothers were close friends.

So, like St. Joseph, I can look back in my own history and see this collaboration prefigured. God is good, provident, and good-humored.

I am honored to appear in these pages with so many contributors I number among my heroes. They come from a wide range of backgrounds and perspectives. Their messages are as varied as their lives. But together they form an integral vision of what it means to be a faithful, faith-filled man in our times, which are no less daunting than the reign of King Herod.

For men living in such times, Joseph is a model, a patron, an intercessor, a companion. His life of silence is instructive because it shows us how God works silently, surprisingly—yet reliably—in our own lives.

By all the titles he's earned—by all the names he has borne—may St. Joseph be invoked today.

Dr. Scott Hahn

Authors' Note

On December 8, 2020, Pope Francis declared 2021 as the Year of St. Joseph. This declaration occurred just days after agreeing to the contract for this book. Carrie and I believe that the timing is not a coincidence but an affirmation from the Holy Spirit that this mission we have been waiting ten years to launch would come to fruition in conjunction with the pope's announcement, and subsequently published during this year dedicated to St. Joseph. We also believe that the timing of you reading this book is not a coincidence but rather an inspired movement of the Holy Spirit, activating you to join us in this mission.

Preface

Carrie

Wiping his shoes as he shuffled through the door, he glanced in my direction. I could tell he was pondering something deeper than the lawn he had just mowed.

"I've been thinking," he began.

I smiled from the other side of the cluttered counter, where I stood arranging the dirty dishes in the washer. It's rare that my husband initiates a conversation with *I've been thinking*. Most interactions start as they end, one long stream of consciousness, words trailing like a tortoise behind the swift hare of his thoughts.

With intense clarity and an irresistible gleam in his eye, Duane continued, "I've been thinking about the state of our nation—our world—and I can clearly see where we have gone wrong. Men are not allowed to be men. If you watch the news or read past the headlines, it's so clear. Men have forsaken virtue and forgotten how to lead. Where did the strong men go? Those leaders who were willing to lay down their lives for the greater good? Look at the mess. *My* mess, the mess of all the men who have failed to do what is right. Men who for decades failed to see their critical role as protector and provider. Am I wrong? Or have we abandoned our post?"

I smiled again. His conviction was compelling. This *man*, who had himself grown up without a father, had eyes to see it. He watched his family struggle with the heartbreaking consequences of abandonment. With the grace of conversion, he recognized the familiar void.

Duane is a good man. He works hours into the night on projects that he did not finish at the office so that he could have dinner with his family. He is a man who wakes up with our hungry baby in the wee hours of the morning. He is a man who sacrificed his promising and cherished military career so our expanding family could move back home. He is a man committed to keeping his primary post.

"This is where we need to exert our efforts," he continued. "The real change needs to start here. Men must stand up and do the right thing. There are faithful brothers, husbands, and fathers out there. We need a voice. Otherwise, our silence is like the abdication of Adam in the garden. We must battle against apathy and fear; we must battle for real manhood. The world needs examples of faithfulness. Someone needs to offer it."

"You received all this while mowing the lawn?" I teased, reaching for his hand and affirming his conviction. "Sounds like you have a book to write. You're being called to encourage other men to keep their sacred post."

This time *he* smiled, and with a nudge, he reminded me that I am the writer in the family.

"We can write it *together*," I countered. "I owe you for all that help with statistics in college."

So here we are. Writing a book . . . together . . . and with other brothers, in Christ, who collectively share this compelling conviction.

Duane

I am not a perfect man, father, or husband. I am nowhere close. I struggle every day. With all the joys that come from a large family, there are daily opportunities for stress. Financial strain, exhaustion, endless chores; did I mention the financial burden?

Over the years, there have been more sleepless nights than I wish to count. I worried about making ends meet or even how to get through another month. Those anxieties easily spilled over to interactions with Carrie and our kids. I constantly felt like I was falling short in my role as husband, father, provider, and protector.

After losing my job, our savings, and nearly our home, I had to face these anxieties head on. What I learned was that in the same way God provided for Joseph in his times of uncertainty, he also provided for me. It took growing in obedience, courage, faithfulness, and patience on my part. When things became difficult, I had to cling to God's grace and stand and fight for my family. Slowly, this daily obedience bore fruit. After months of feeling like a failure, I began to experience a greater freedom in my vocation. God knew where he was leading us. His only condition was that I rely on him and not abandon my post in the process. Over time, I felt strengthened in my faith, in our marriage, and in our family, which gave me the courage to man my post. Don't get me wrong, occasionally I still lose sleep, but those nights are a lot less frequent.

Without a father to look up to, I have always been drawn to St. Joseph. I have a deep affinity towards him. In him, I see a tremendously strong and resolute man that risked everything for Mary and Jesus. Talk about being called into a stressful situation. Your future bride is pregnant with the Son of God, and you are called (in a dream) to take care of them. I don't know about you, but I would not be sleeping soundly enough to dream with the stress and burden that he carried. Yet, St. Joseph does not run, he does not make excuses, he does not look for the easy way out. Instead, he faces it head on. He becomes the earthly father and the example to all men for how we should bear our responsibilities and risk everything for those in our care.

However, when it comes to the man who risked everything to be a father to the Son of God, not much is recorded about him. Joseph was presumably with Jesus almost all the time. He would have had a profound impact on our Savior. I can imagine both of them in Joseph's workshop together, working side by side, as I do with my own children. There is something sacred about this time together. Jesus would have learned so much about being a man from his earthly father.

Despite St. Joseph's profound influence, we Catholics are still a little cloudy on where he fits into our faith. While recently putting our youngest son, William Joseph, to bed, he humorously reinforced this reality. His nightly routine that week was to list all those who love him. After listing our family, he rounded out the long list with Jesus and Mary. We gently reminded him not to forget his patron, St. Joseph, to which he wondered aloud, "Who is that?"

"Mary's husband. The head of the Holy Family," Carrie explained, trying to jog his four-year-old memory.

"Oh, that guy," Will replied with a drowsy sigh.

Oh, that guy.

Like my son, most of us have heard about St. Joseph, but we don't really *know* him. Yes, we see him every Christmas quietly kneeling in front of the plastic manger wearing his humble tunic, sitting across from his well-composed wife, who does not look at all like she just gave birth. Beyond that, we struggle to explain him. *Oh, St. Joseph, he is the guy who was Mary's husband even though she is a virgin. I mean, he is Jesus's father, but not his real father.*

Our limited understanding seems to fall terribly short. Joseph is the patron saint of the Universal Church, the patron saint of fathers, the patron of workers and of families—to just name a few! As head of the Holy Family, St. Joseph's role is vital. His leadership protected our Mother and guided our Savior. While it is understandable that we struggle to explain him, it is now time that we get to know him. In a world in need of strong men, St. Joseph is *the Man* who leads the way.

Moving Through This Book

For years, I have benefited from the protection of St. Joseph. Every time I struggled with work, started a new endeavor, or had a child, St. Joseph showed up offering extraordinary protection and timely intervention. His enduring example of masculine virtue is outlined in the Litany of St. Joseph, which is the backbone of this book. Each merit offers a small glimpse into the virtue modeled by this silent saint. Practices that offer ordinary men like you and me a roadmap to follow, leading us on an extraordinary mission.

To offer this roadmap, we have enlisted the help of Catholic leaders—faithful, strong men who have stories to tell and wisdom to share as they have struggled through life's challenges and learned to adopt the virtues of St. Joseph.

Each chapter begins with a quotation from St. John Paul II that relates to the virtues inherent in St. Joseph's life. Sharing an admiration and love for St. Joseph, St. John Paul II is the virtuous patron of our family's ministry: The John Paul II Healing Center.[1] Following each quotation is an intro-

---

[1]   The John Paul II Healing Center was founded by Carrie's dad, and fellow contributor, Dr. Bob Schuchts. Carrie serves as a presenter for many of the center's events, while Duane has served as a long-time business consultant for the ministry. The Healing Center serves priests, religious, and lay people through healing conferences, retreats, and resources.

ductory overview of each particular virtue and a relatable testimony by a man who has found encouragement in the example of St. Joseph in his roles as a husband, father, son, brother, priest, or protector. Included at the end of each chapter are questions for reflection, a *Mobilizing the Mission* challenge, and a prayer for living out that specific virtue.

This book is not a resource; it is a mission, our mission. Flanked with a new band of brothers, it is time to fulfill your calling and *man your post*!

Litany of St. Joseph

Lord, have mercy on us. Christ, have mercy on us.
Lord, have mercy on us.
Jesus, hear us, Jesus, graciously hear us.

God the Father of heaven, have mercy on us.
God the Son, Redeemer of the World, have mercy on us.
God the Holy Spirit, have mercy on us.
Holy Trinity, one God, have mercy on us.

Holy Mary, pray for us.
St. Joseph, pray for us.
Renowned offspring of David, pray for us.
Light of Patriarchs, pray for us.
Spouse of the Mother of God, pray for us.
Chaste guardian of the Virgin, pray for us.
Foster father of the Son of God, pray for us.
Diligent protector of Christ, pray for us.
Head of the Holy Family, pray for us.
Joseph most just, pray for us.
Joseph most chaste, pray for us.
Joseph most prudent, pray for us.
Joseph most courageous, pray for us.
Joseph most obedient, pray for us.
Joseph most faithful, pray for us.

Mirror of patience, pray for us.
Lover of poverty, pray for us.
Model of workers, pray for us.
Glory of home life, pray for us.
Guardian of virgins, pray for us.
Pillar of families, pray for us.
Comfort of the troubled, pray for us.
Hope of the sick, pray for us.
Patron of the dying, pray for us.
Terror of demons, pray for us.
Protector of Holy Church, pray for us.

Lamb of God, who takes away the sins of the world, spare us, O Jesus.
Lamb of God, who takes away the sins of the world, graciously hear us, O Jesus.
Lamb of God, who takes away the sins of the world, have mercy on us, O Jesus.

He made him the lord of his household, and prince over all his possessions.
Let us pray:
O God, in your ineffable providence you were pleased to choose Blessed Joseph to be the spouse of your most holy Mother; grant, we beg you, that we may be worthy to have him for our intercessor in heaven whom on earth we venerate as our Protector: You who live and reign forever and ever.
Saint Joseph, pray for us.

CHAPTER I

Joseph Most Just

"Being a just man . . . he [Joseph] wishes to dissolve his marriage in a loving way. The angel of the Lord tells him that would not be consistent with his vocation; indeed it would be contrary to the spousal love uniting him to Mary."[1]

—Pope St. John Paul II

Joseph was a just man. How do we know? Because the Bible tells us so. Verbatim. Scripture, which is thin on details of the great saint, explicitly tells us that Joseph was just. Justice, one of the four theological virtues, was an inherent quality in creation. In the beginning, man was created with what Pope St. John Paul II refers to as a state of original justice.[2] This means that original man, wholly integrated as a person, ordered everything to the glory of God and the good of every creature.

---

[1] Pope John Paul II, "Letter to Families," February 2, 1994, http://www.vatican.va/content/john-paul-ii/en/letters/1994/documents/hf_jp-ii_let_02021994_families.html.

[2] Pope John Paul II, "The Mystery of Man's Original Innocence," General Audience, January 30, 1980.

The first man and woman, Adam and Eve, forfeited this justice through sin and rebellion. But the *Fairest Love*[3] between Joseph and Mary helped to restore God's justice. In refusing to subject Mary to shame, Joseph pledges friendship to God and creation. He practices the moral virtue that consists of the "constant and firm will to give their due to God and neighbor."[4]

Each of us are challenged by Joseph's example of justice. In his witness as head of the Holy Family, Joseph modeled this virtue for Jesus. As Jesus grew, he witnessed the tender and righteous acts of his earthly father through the trusting relationship Joseph had with God. As Joseph followed the heavenly Father's promptings, God led the Holy Family into uncharted territories. Jesus also witnessed Joseph's love of neighbor as he cherished Mary by living out their chaste love. Jesus knew justice because he experienced it firsthand in his school of love, his family. Steeped in virtue and one with the Father's will, Jesus knew who he was and what he was called to do.

As you read this chapter on justice, Mike will share his story of learning to live justly with the help of many holy examples. The imperfect but wholehearted devotion that he witnessed modeled for him the *Fairest Love* of Joseph and Mary. In return, Mike ordered his life *to the glory of God and the good of every creature* and has become a model of justice for many.

While you read his testimony, I encourage you to contemplate your own life experiences. Is your life ordered to the glory of God? Where are you on the journey toward justice?

---

3   Pope John Paul II, "Letter to Families."
4   *Catechism of the Catholic Church* 1807.

At the end of this chapter, there will be opportunity for reflection, prayer, and a challenge to accept your mission so that you may experience deeper blessing and restoration in your own journey toward becoming a just man, like Joseph (and Mike).

Step Up to the Plate

Mike Sweeney

My father was my first hero. He was a *just* man like St. Joseph. He is one of a handful of holy examples of righteous men in my life. These holy men have modeled sacrifice and personified justice. They have offered me direction in my own journey to becoming a just man, like St. Joseph.

My journey began on July 22, 1973. On the night of my birth, my dad put a baseball bat next to me in the incubator and sat outside the hospital all night, tearfully praying for a miracle. As an aspiring Major League Baseball player with the California Angels, my dad gave up his aspirations of playing in the big leagues to raise his family. He sacrificed his dreams so that we could live ours. As the second of eight children born to Mike and Maureen Sweeney, I was two months premature and weighed only four pounds. The doctors told my parents that I only had a 50 percent chance of survival.

My mother, a prayer warrior, began praying the Rosary for my life and then asked the hospital to call a priest. "If God is going to call my baby to heaven, please call Fr. O'Connor to come baptize him." I was baptized that day in the hospital. I became a beloved son of God and a member of his holy

Catholic Church. God wrote my name in the Book of Life and called me to be a saint. Fr. O'Conner became the first of many priests in my life who showed me the sacrificial love of Jesus in the sacraments.

The next morning, in the UC Irvine Hospital, only one mile from Angel Stadium where my dad would have played baseball, the doctors informed my parents that their prayers had been answered. Their baby boy was going to live. The connection to angels never left me. I often wonder if an angel appeared to my father that night, like the reassuring angel that appeared to St. Joseph. God had a plan that was bigger than the bleak circumstances that each of these men initially faced.

As a child, my parents built a home around our Catholic faith. Our growing family never missed Sunday Mass. My parents taught us that Sunday was made for the family to go to Mass together, to receive Jesus in the Eucharist, and then to come home for a grand slam breakfast cooked by mother's hands. My mom was the greatest example of the Blessed Mother modeling holiness, modesty, humility, and a great love for Jesus. My father exemplified strength, hard work, humility, faith, and the selflessness of St. Joseph every single day. Growing up, I always said that I wanted to be a man like my father, and I wanted to marry a woman like my mother. We didn't have too many material possessions, but I felt like we were rich beyond earthly measure. I once heard this sentiment summed up in these perfect words: "The rich man is not the man who has the most; it is the man who needs the least." My parents made sure we were never in need.

When I was seventeen years old, I was drafted by the

Kansas City Royals and reported to Baseball City, Florida. This was the first test of my faith outside the umbrella of my parents' love. On that first Sunday, there was no question that I was going to Mass. Even while my teammates slept in or went to the beach, I looked in the phone book to find a church. I found that St. Ann Catholic Church in Haines City had Mass at 9 a.m. I begged one of my teammates, who was headed to the beach, to drop me off at church. I paid him three bucks in gas money for the ride.

God was at work because I encountered another example of St. Joseph at St. Ann Catholic Church, Fr. Domingo Gonzalez. Father Domingo had left communist Cuba to bring Christ to the people in the United States. After the 9 a.m. Mass, Fr. Domingo engaged me in conversation. I told him that I was new with the Royals and didn't have a ride back to the baseball complex. He told me that if I could wait until after the 10:30 a.m. Spanish Mass, he would give me a ride. I happily accepted his offer. Before I climbed out of his car, Fr. Domingo said, "Mijo, I will pick you up at 7:30 a.m. next Sunday." When I asked why so early for 9 a.m. Mass, he said, "We will have breakfast and fellowship before Mass. After the Spanish Mass, we will have lunch and I will bring you back." What a special time that was for me. Each Sunday, I attended two Masses and had fellowship and formation with a holy priest! I later found out that my parents were praying for God to send me an angel. Fr. Domingo was that angel.

On September 4, 1995, I made my major league debut. However, I soon realized that my career was not going as I had planned. Heading into spring training in 1999, there were rumors going around that my time with the Royals was nearing an end. I approached my manager, Tom Burgmeier, to ask if this was true. He told me, "Son, you have zero chance of making the team this year." This ton of bricks hit me on Ash Wednesday, February 17, 1999. I went to the Church of the Nativity in Overland Park to pray. My heartbreak turned into tears. I had hit rock bottom. As I was praying, I was drawn to a sticker on my Bible of a tandem bicycle. God asked me, "Have you truly placed Jesus in the center of your life, on the front seat of your tandem bike?" Then I clearly heard, "You need to get on the back seat, simply trust in Me, and pedal your heart out!" At once I had peace, recalling the words of Philippians 4:7, "And the peace of God, which surpasses all understanding, will guard your hearts and minds in Christ Jesus." I hadn't felt that kind of peace in a long time. That night, I surrendered my life completely to Christ. With the consolation of the Lord, I felt the call to live justly for the Lord. This commitment included the decision to practice purity and prepare myself for either marriage or the priesthood.

That night was transforming. I found a new freedom in Christ that allowed me to relax and perform like an all-star on the field and a saint-in-the-making off the field. I became consumed with Christ and immersed in the Holy Bible. Success followed. I not only made the Royals team that year but went on to play in five Major League Baseball All-Star games and was eventually inducted into the Kansas City Royals Hall of Fame in 2015.

My commitment to purity was not without challenges and persecution. One day in 2001, while on a team bus ride, one of my teammates shouted to me, in front of the whole team, "I have been on this team for two years and I have never seen you date a girl. Tonight, after the game, I saw a beautiful girl hanging over the dugout with a sign that said, 'All I want for my birthday is Mike Sweeney.' Then I saw you crumble up the paper with her phone number. What's wrong with you Sweeney? Are you gay?"

Even though I turned red with rage and I wanted to fight, I heard the words in my heart, "Be still, and know that I am God" (Ps 46:10). Despite my great embarrassment, I was proud that I could quietly bear this affliction for Christ. In the ensuing days, as we would shake hands with teammates after a win, I still wanted to rip this teammate's arm off with each shake.

Then one day, in my role as team chapel leader, I gathered my teammates for chapel. I went around the locker room and invited everyone on my team, intentionally skipping over my teammate who had embarrassed me on the bus. As I passed him over, he said to me, "Hey Sween-Dog! Aren't you going to invite me to chapel today?"

I responded, "Brother, why should I waste my breath. I have invited you every Sunday over the past two years and you have never come. Why should I invite you today?"

"Well, maybe today was going to be my first day coming to chapel," he replied, then gestured to speak with me privately. "Sweens, are you upset with me?"

"Yes, absolutely I am upset with you! You broke my heart in front of my teammates. Man, I lived a life I wasn't proud of for a long time, but God called me to live a life of chastity and purity as a Catholic Christian."

With tears in his eyes he said, "Sweens, I am really sorry

for what I said. I am married with three children and I wish I had the faith you have. Will you forgive me?"

Reconciled, we gave each other a big hug and went into the chapel together. That day an amazing friendship was formed.

Living justly eventually had its tangible reward off the field. Early in my career, I had met the daughter of former major league player Jim Nettles, who was our bullpen coach in Kansas City. Shara Nettles was someone I could see myself with, but I knew I was not ready for marriage at that early stage in my career, so Shara and I parted ways. Thankfully, we met again in 2001 in her hometown of Seattle, where my second MLB All-Star game was held. All those years of living in chastity seemed to prepare my heart for this moment.

At a special family dinner after the Home Run Derby, I invited Shara to join us. When I saw this radiant woman walk into the restaurant, I jumped from my chair and hugged her as if I never wanted it to end. I felt the Holy Spirit say, "This is the one I have been preparing you for over the past couple of years, the one you have been praying for." Pushing my brother Richard out of the chair next to me, I asked Shara to sit with me at dinner. That night, I realized she was the one I had been waiting for. We were engaged within six months, and nine months later, I married my soulmate.

Shara was the spouse God had chosen for me and he could not have chosen a better one. She is everything I ever dreamed of, and then some. I found a partner for life, a holy, modest, beautiful, and humble woman like my mother. Together, we have been completely open to life. We are overjoyed with our three boys and three girls, ranging from ages one to sixteen.

Faith is at the center of our family life. One of my favorite things to do is to wake up early and cook breakfast for the kids (to give Shara a break). Once the children are driven to their respective Catholic schools, Shara and I take Ryan Burke, our youngest, to daily Mass. In the evening, we pray the Rosary as a family. I believe that our prayer time together is what makes our family clock tick. We also encourage our kids to pray from the heart so that they can have a personal relationship with Jesus. Our children know that we are not as interested in their earthly success as we are in their eternal joy. While my boys want to be professional baseball players like their dad, they also know I will love them even if they never play another game of baseball. We want them to be faithful followers of Jesus first and foremost.

God has been so gracious to me and has blessed me more than I deserve. He has graced me with the gift of faith in his Son, the gift of marrying a holy woman like my mother and having six children with her, who are living life with their eyes fixed on eternity. As a family, we seek holiness through the indwelling of the Holy Spirt that came upon us at Baptism, fueled with Jesus in the Eucharist in Holy Mass and surrounded by a faith-filled community. My deepest desire is to help my spouse and children get to heaven by providing for them, praying with them, teaching them, protecting them, and guiding them in the ways of faith. My life is an ongoing journey to become a just man, like St. Joseph. I want to be a saint, not so that I am remembered by the Church, but so that I can live eternity with Jesus in heaven. Baseball is what I did, but a follower of Jesus is who I am. My primary vocation is to lead my family along the same path to justice in the footsteps of my father and the many holy priests I have encountered along the way (Fr. Domingo, Fr. Martin Latiff, Fr. Burke Masters, and others). I know my parents hit a home run through their example of faith. As for me, I will never stop swinging for the fences.

St. Joseph, Most Just, *pray for us!*

Engaging the Message

1. Pray with the following passage from Psalm 37:27–28.

   > "Depart from evil, and do good;
   >   so shall you abide for ever.
   > For the LORD loves justice;
   >   he will not forsake his saints."

   - Read the Scripture passage once and become familiar with the text.
   - Slowly read the passage a second time.
   - Very, very slowly read the passage a third time, paying attention to the words and phrases that rest in your heart. What is God speaking to you through this passage?

2. What men in your life have exemplified the virtue of justice?
3. What choices have they made that you admired?
4. How has their example inspired you to live more justly?

Mobilizing the Mission

If there is a man in your life (father, brother, teacher, coach, priest, or friend) that exemplifies justice, thank him for his holy example.

Closing Prayer

Heavenly Father, thank you for sending your son, Jesus, our Savior, to restore righteousness and reconcile us to you. Please forgive me for all the times I failed to act justly, clinging to evil desires instead of your just promises. Please, reveal any places of disorder in my life. I give you permission to order my desires and convict me of wrongdoing. By your grace, grant me the courage to act justly and become a man with a heart like St. Joseph. Amen.

————————

Mike Sweeney is a five-time Major League Baseball All-Star first baseman and was inducted into Kansas City Royals Hall of Fame in 2015. He now works as a special assistant to the GM for the Kansas City Royals and also is the founder of Catholic Baseball Camps and the San Diego Saints Baseball where he "uses the greatest game ever played to share the Greatest Story ever told." Mike is a practicing Catholic and daily communicant who speaks around the world about his love for Jesus and his holy Catholic Church. Mike has been married to his wife, Shara, for over eighteen years, and they are blessed with six children.

CHAPTER 2

Joseph Most Chaste

"Only the chaste man and the chaste women are capable of real love."[1]

—Pope St. John Paul II

Chastity—a word that seems to have lost its meaning in a culture saturated with sex. Chastity is often viewed as an outdated and old-fashioned ideal, a concept reserved for innocent young maidens who lived in days of yore, and certainly not a label most men boast about in the locker room.

But here we have St. Joseph, a man given the title of Most Chaste Spouse. Of all the titles given to the great saint, this one is reserved for the Eucharistic Prayer uttered at nearly every Mass. While most men cannot conceive of a marriage without sex, St. Joseph answered that call. A model for husbands and priests, Joseph embraced both marriage and celibacy in one call. His life embodied the vocations of

---

[1]   Karol Wojtyla, *Love and Responsibility* (Boston: Pauline Books and Media 2013), 171.

masculinity like no other. His pledge of chastity illuminates the call for both married and religious men.

His pledge is your pledge. Did you know that in baptism you became a model of chastity too? All Christ's faithful are called to lead a chaste life. We make this pledge at the moment of our baptism.[2] This means that *chaste* is your title too.

This does not make the choice of chastity synonymous with a vow of celibacy. Nor does it mean we are all called to embrace celibacy, as St. Joseph did. It means that single men and women are completely capable of chaste love. Married men and women are capable of sexually intimate chaste love. Conversely, married or religious men who refrain from sexual intimacy are still capable of sexual sin in their unchaste thoughts or actions.

Therefore, chastity is not fundamentally about refraining or abstaining from sex. It is foremost about integration. "The chaste person maintains the integrity of the powers of life and love placed in him. This integrity ensures the unity of the person; it is opposed to any behavior that would impair it. It tolerates neither a double life nor duplicity of speech."[3] St. Joseph was the Most Chaste Spouse because he was completely integrated as a person and understood the sublimity of his mission: Upholding the purity of Mary, the undefiled Ark of the New Covenant.

Another way the Church defines chastity is an "apprenticeship in self-mastery."[4] St. John Paul II emphasizes that true masculine strength is controlling your impulses instead

---

[2]   *Catechism of the Catholic Church* 2348.
[3]   *CCC* 2338.
[4]   *CCC* 2339.

of being controlled by them. This means that Joseph experienced the freedom of true love, which can only flourish with purity of heart.[5]

Your passage toward chastity is your own apprenticeship in self-mastery. It is the mode of authentic masculine integrity and strength. As you read about Andrew's journey toward self-mastery, call to mind the times you have grown in masculine strength or cowered as you wrestled with this virtue. Reflect specifically on how it makes you feel when you are controlled by your passions versus how you feel when you uphold the call to love freely.

Triumph Over Shame

Andrew Laubacher

I distinctly remember the first time I looked at porn. I was in eighth grade and a "friend" smuggled a magazine in his shoe to show me in the bathroom during recess. Twenty years have passed, and the memory is forever fixed in my mind. I felt sick, scared, unsettled. While I knew this topless woman was a real person, not just a picture, an unfamiliar feeling began to brew in my heart and I had no idea what to do with it.

I encountered this same feeling again a year later when my friends introduced me to hardcore porn. I was quickly indoctrinated into the world of sexual sin. I bought into the lie that chastity was boring and that sexual adventure was

---

5   Pope John Paul II, "Truth Rooted in Man's Original Innocence," General Audience, April 1, 1981.

exciting and using women was gratifying. I pursued all these pleasures in the name of freedom and good fun.

Growing up in a faith-filled Catholic home, I went to Mass every Sunday and attended many Catholic youth retreats and camps, and I served for a time as an altar boy. Both of my parents came from large Catholic families. They were amazing parents, loving and present. My older sister and I had a great upbringing. I loved surfing, music, sports, and hanging with friends. Yet none of that could prepare me for the combination of constant peer pressure and the revolution of the internet. Although my body and soul longed for love and intimacy, I was bound by the culture and an all-consuming desire to fit in.

After switching from a Catholic grade school to attend a public high school, I found myself immersed in an unfamiliar environment. I was instantly exposed to a culture where religion was for the weak and freedom was found in sexual liberation. Slowly, it became my reality. I frequented parties, I smoked weed, I tried alcohol, and I became absorbed in porn and sexual fantasies. My life became a constant pursuit of hookups and sexual conquests, later boasted about in the locker room.

It was during this time that I began to question my Catholic faith. Bombarded with worldly pleasure, I chose the world. I didn't want to be that prudish, weird religious guy. Viewing porn with my friends became a regular occurrence. I became addicted. I couldn't stop.

It never crossed my mind that I was sinning. I wasn't killing anyone, right? As the years of high school passed by, I continued my venture into practical atheism and unbelief.

While I still attended retreats, the voices of the everyday world seemed to choke out the periodic voices of truth in the Church.

As much as I focused on sexual pursuits, I found myself feeling like I could not compete with my six-foot jock friends that found sexual conquests to be quite easy. While I ran with the popular crowd, I was much smaller than many of my friends. I was only 5'5" and weighed 110 pounds. I did not like my body and struggled with feeling insecure. All my friends were having sex regularly; I was not. I was only able to get so far. This sexual frustration led me to look at more porn. I thought it was the thing to do. I thought I was living a life of freedom. In truth, I was becoming bound by the slavery of lust and anger.

Surprisingly, during all that time partying and pursuing girls, I never technically had sexual intercourse with anyone. I could tell you some funny stories about how these potential encounters were thwarted. Ultimately, I believe God was protecting me from going *all the way* with someone. He had another design for my life, one that I couldn't see while living in the ways of the world, plans that included traveling around the world leading worship, preaching the gospel, sharing the gift of chastity with others, and eventually entering seminary to begin studies for the priesthood.

So what was the shift? What happened that this depressed, angry, ashamed boy grew up to pursue true sexual freedom? That is another *funny* story. A few weeks after graduation, I found myself driving to my usual party house after teaching a summer surf lesson and getting high with a coworker. On the way, I was pulled over by a cop. Since I was in possession of drugs, I was arrested and forced to appear in court. I had to stand in front of a judge in all my shame and pay a hefty fine. This humiliation scared the *you know what* out of me. My parents were disappointed and terribly hurt by my actions. It was then that I knew I did not want to live that life anymore.

That summer, I abruptly stopped partying. My so-called friends stopped hanging out with me because I didn't want to party. This drastic shift exasperated the anxiety I already suffered. I began to have horrible panic attacks. I blamed God. I was depressed, anxious, and questioning. Then it happened. I was invited to a Steubenville Youth Conference, and my encounter with the Holy Spirit transformed my life.

After that retreat, unlike the countless others I had attended over the years, I left desiring sainthood. I wanted to learn about Jesus and the Church he had started. I began to read and watch everything I could on the existence of God. I began to find that the Catholic Church had amazing answers to the questions of the human heart. During this time of great fervor for the gospel, I stopped listening to all my rap and rock 'n' roll music and started praying with praise and worship music. I dove into youth ministry and began playing guitar and eventually leading a worship band.

While I longed for the spiritual, I still struggled with the carnal. The addiction I experienced in high school did not go away. Naively, I believed that once I repented and gave my life to Jesus, all my problems would vanish. I had stopped smoking and drinking immediately after that retreat and began to go to confession regularly. However, the lust remained. I realized the imminent need to address and properly order my sexuality. I could no longer act on every sexual impulse. I wondered where I would even begin.

I began to realize this was going to be a hard-fought battle. It is a battle that all men must fight. I am still learning that there is freedom *in* the battle. I don't have to have all the answers. Honestly, I have failed thousands of times. The only difference I experienced after encountering the grace of conversion was knowing this was not God's plan for me. This was not his plan for human sexuality. So I ran to confession! I can't tell you how many confessions I have been to for lust, but every time I walk out of that confessional, I begin anew with God's grace to fight for purity again. It has been a struggle since the first day I gave my life to Jesus. I struggled with masturbation, and it took many years to be free of my porn addiction. This cycle of shame and guilt was often haunting. Sometimes the shame was too overwhelming to bear. I could hear Satan tell me *I'm not worthy of love* and that *I will never be free*. That was not the voice of truth.

If you have experienced sexual mistakes, abuse, and addiction, immerse yourself in the Divine Mercy of Jesus Christ. Contrary to popular belief, the Church is not here to make us feel guilty. We are sexual beings. The world talks about sex all the time. The Church must talk about sex too. We must talk about the beauty and strength found in sexual wholeness. In these conversations, I have learned that I am not my sexual desire. This means you are not your sexual desire either. There is so much more to us than that. Reducing ourselves to our sexual experience or preference is not of God. No matter if we are single, married, or celibate, we are made to practice chastity. Every vocation demands it.

How do we live it? First, I found I needed consistent prayer and meditation. I discovered the sacraments, the Rosary, devotions, and novenas to be powerful spiritual tools. I have also found freedom in serving others. Living a life of faith and fellowship within my community connects me with real people, not just screens. Snapchat and Instagram do not count! I began to cultivate friendships rooted in Christ. This was essential. While porn is usually viewed in a dark room alone, the light of Christ requires me to bring my struggles into the light. When any of us struggle, the best thing to do is tell someone. The Catholic Church should be the safest place to turn. Here, we have access to freedom in reconciliation.

As important as those practices have been, I have also found that if I just focus on the spiritual, I cannot remain free. The truth is I never trained myself to exercise self-control. I needed to learn how to grow in virtue. That wasn't something I had ever seen on my twitter feed. An Army Ranger once told me after an event I played in New York, "If you seek comfort, you will deprive yourself of self-knowledge." I had to learn who I was before I could understand what I was here for. With God's grace, I have made great progress. I began to implement practices to arm me in the battle. God's grace builds on nature. My job was then to strengthen my weaknesses and cooperate with grace.

This cooperation required some real changes. Along with all these spiritual practices, I got a filtration program on all my devices. I also found that an accountability partner was essential. I was convinced that I needed to use my body for good. With exercise, eating well, getting good sleep, and giving up excessive alcohol, I began to feel better about myself.

Since nothing good happens late at night, I stopped binge watching Netflix till 4 a.m. I also kept a gratitude journal. Every morning, I would jot down three things I was grateful for. Lastly, I would find ways to deny myself. I found two small ways to practice self-control each day. For me that took the form of a cold shower or saying no to that second beer.

Right now, you may be shaking your head, thinking, "Andrew, if I do those things, I will lead a sad, depressed life." No! You will be free! I want us to be free together. When we exercise the muscle and virtue of saying no to little things, we can say no to sexual sin and yes to freedom and real love! I have experienced this freedom firsthand. Skilled athletes would never compete without hard fought, intense training. Obtaining success requires our sacrifice.

Ultimately, I learned to persevere. While I am certainly not perfect, I won't let Satan keep me down. Proverbs tells us, "For a righteous man falls seven times, and rises again" (Prv 24:16). We must not give up! I am still here only because God's grace has allowed me to keep getting back up. You have access to that same grace. Get back up, run to confession, run back to the Father's loving arms. The Church doesn't want us to be a bored prude sitting around feeling sexually repressed all day. Chastity leads to the greatest freedom a soul will ever obtain. It is worth the fight. Start today. I will be fighting with you. Let us turn to St. Joseph, Mary's most chaste spouse, and ask for his intercession as we love God and others, bringing the freedom of Christ everywhere we go.

Joseph, Most Chaste, *pray for us!*

Engaging the Message

1. Pray with the following passage from 1 Corinthians
    6:18.

    "Shun immorality. Every other sin which a man
    commits is outside the body; but the immoral
    man sins against his own body."

    *   Read the Scripture passage once and become familiar
        with the text.
    *   Slowly read the passage a second time.
    *   Very, very slowly read the passage a third time,
        paying attention to the words and phrases that rest
        in your heart. What is God speaking to you through
        this passage?

2. What sexual sins have you struggled with? Be honest
    with yourself.
3. How have you grown in chastity over the years?
4. What measures are you willing to take to live a more
    integrated, chaste life? List these measures here.

Mobilizing the Mission

Confess a current or past struggle with sexual sin in the confessional this week. Deeply receive Christ's divine mercy.
If you are currently struggling with a sexual compulsion,
addiction, or fantasy, find someone equipped to journey
with you. Integration begins with facing our weakness and
seeking help in our vocation.

Closing Prayer

Heavenly Father, thank you for the gift of my body and my holy desire and longing for intimacy and communion. I ask for your forgiveness for all the specific ways (list struggles here) I have misused the body you have given me. I also ask forgiveness for all the times I used or objectified others (list examples here). Bless my sexuality and masculinity and create in me a clean and integrated heart. I pray for a new longing to experience chaste love, real love, like St. Joseph.

———————

Andrew Laubacher (ALOB) graduated from Franciscan University with a degree in Theology and currently attends Seminary at St. John Seminary in Camarillo, California where he is discerning a call to the priesthood. Andrew is a songwriter, musician, and speaker who travels the world leading worship and evangelizing young people. Andrew has released an album (*No Match for Love*) and two singles. To contact Andrew or purchase his music go to Alobmusic.com

CHAPTER 3

Joseph Most Prudent

*"The beginnings of our redemption were entrusted to the
faithful care of Joseph. . . . God placed him at the head of
his family, as a faithful and prudent servant so that with
fatherly care he may watch over his only begotten son."*[1]

—Pope St. John Paul II

Imagine St. Joseph arriving in Bethlehem, exhausted after
days of traveling, only to realize his wife was in full-blown
labor and there was not a single vacant room in the entire
town. He must have entertained doubts about his decision
to caravan straight through to Jerusalem, refusing to veer off
an exit or two earlier in Jericho. If he carried any expectation
that the trip home from Bethlehem would be less eventful,
his two-year detour to Egypt certainly shattered that belief.
It is safe to say that most men in St. Joseph's position would
have been tempted to turn back or abandon the plan. Joseph,

---

[1] Pope John Paul II, *Redemptoris Custos*, Apostolic Exhortation, August
15, 1989, http://www.vatican.va/content/john-paul-ii/en/apost_
exhortations/documents/hf_jp-ii_exh_15081989_redemptoris
-custos.html.

deeply grounded in accomplishing the God-given task, persevered under trying conditions. Relying on the wisdom of the wise men and the prophetic voice of an angel, Joseph faithfully carried out this sacred mission.

St. Joseph practiced prudence, "the virtue that disposes practical reason to discern our true good in every circumstance and to choose the right means of achieving it."[2] Prudence is the key for the accomplishment of the fundamental task that each of us has received from God.[3] Prudence is the right means to achieving a good, and it requires discernment and forethought. Each decision Christian men make should be rooted in something deeper than temporary or fleeting feelings. Instead, decisions must be measured by the greatest good; additionally, prudent decision-making should not be mistaken for fear or indecisiveness. St. Joseph practiced this virtue with extraordinary courage. Immense resolution is required to rank reason and wisdom over urge and impulse. Prudence helps to anchor our decisions long after they are made, particularly when things get difficult and doubts creep in. Prudence lights the way.

As you read Justin's story, pay attention to the ways he struggled without an understanding of this virtue and how he eventually learned to embrace it. Also, call to mind the times you have struggled in the practice of prudence. Ask the Holy Spirit to reveal places in your life where you are being called to better embrace this virtue.

---

[2]   *Catechism of the Catholic Church* 1806.

[3]   Pope John Paul II, General Audience, October 25, 1978, http://www.vatican.va/content/john-paul-ii/en/audiences/1978/documents/hf_jp-ii_aud_19781025.html.

Seek Wise Counsel

Justin Biance

I was seven years old the first time I washed dishes. I remember the night clearly. Our family had just finished dinner and my dad asked me, my brother, and my sister to join him on the couch. I knew something was wrong because my mom stayed behind clearing the table in the kitchen. Once all three of us kids were sitting, my dad informed us that he and my mom were getting a divorce and he was moving out. My sister began to cry, and my brother and I sat speechless trying to grasp every word he spoke after the initial blow. When my dad was finished, he stood up and walked out. As soon as the door closed behind him, my mom rushed in from the other room. As she consoled my sister and addressed the three of us, I could not hear a word she uttered. It was as if she was on mute. Dazed, I stood up and walked into the kitchen. Through the small window above the sink, I watched my dad's headlights disappear into the night. The pain I felt was completely unfamiliar. The reality of what happened hit me hard. I didn't know what to do. Instead of letting my mom see me cry, I grabbed a dish and started washing.

The sting that I felt in my heart that night was the sting of fatherlessness. I didn't have words for my emotions at the time, but for the first time in my life, I felt insecure, alone, and ill-equipped to handle anything. Without dad around, I wondered if I would be safe and if I would make good decisions. More than any of that, I wondered who would take care of us.

Over the next several years, I began to identify as the *man of the house*. I bought into the world's standard of manhood. Conforming to the *self-made* image, I learned to play sports and to fix things without my dad. As for the stuff that I simply did not know how to do? I mimicked my friends. Scripture tells us, "He who walks with wise men becomes wise" (Prv 13:20). Looking back, I realize the void left by my father was a void of wisdom and prudence guiding my life.

Once I finished high school, I moved to Tallahassee to attend Florida State University (FSU). After a few months of becoming acquainted with my surroundings, a friend from back home invited me to attend a meeting at church. I was hesitant but went anyway. I walked into a room filled with music and singing and very happy people. It was the strangest thing. The group was the Catholic Student Union. While I was Catholic, I had never encountered a group like this. I decided to hang out in the back of the room for a few minutes and then discreetly exit at the first opportunity. Seemingly out of nowhere, a man approached me and introduced himself, "Hi, I'm Brother Sam, what's your name?" At this point, my feeling of awkwardness had reached new heights, but I politely greeted him and, in the end, discovered that I enjoyed our brief conversation.

That conversation led to many more conversations. It also led to me to the acquaintance of other holy men such as Dr. Bob Schuchts, Dr. Tom Neal, Monsignor Slade Crawford, and an entire community called the Brotherhood of Hope. Over the course of my four years at FSU, these men fathered me, mentored me, and taught me about the Catholic faith. Through these men, my vision for fatherhood was restored.

This challenged me to begin to look at my life differently. Almost overnight, my choices meant something. Men who exhibited prudence in their daily actions were mentoring me, and I wanted to be like that; I wanted to be like them. I began the arduous task of turning away from years of habitual sin. Without these holy examples in my life, I would not have even tried. Their wisdom guided me through difficult decisions such as ending harmful relationships and even reconciling with my dad. Leaning on their fatherhood and wisdom gave me the courage to begin a lifelong journey to love and imitate Christ.

After graduation, I married my college sweetheart, Angela, and we began our life together. Around that time, I took a job at the Boy Scouts of America, which helped deepen my thinking about brotherhood and fatherhood. The contrast of two distinct seasons of my life, high school and college, were constantly on my mind. In high school, I suffered with sin and confusion. In college, I turned away from sin and began pursuing virtue. As I worked for the character building rite of passage program for young men, it all became clear. I realized when I was surrounded by virtuous men in college, I thrived. This reflection inspired a vision for starting a Catholic program for young men that would answer this need for mentoring boys. After a few years of prayer, discernment, and conversations with friends and mentors, I founded an organization called Fraternus.

Launching Fraternus was exciting. My dear friend, Thomas Van Horn, quit graduate school to travel the country and raise money for this vision, which only existed in a business plan. After we received our first generous donation,

I quit my job to focus on Fraternus full-time. I was twenty-five years old and had a mortgage and two children at the time, but with six months of expenses in the freshly opened Fraternus bank account, I was all set! Tommy and I continued to develop the vision, and I hired a local youth director, Jason Craig, to take the lead in building out the program content. By the end of the second year, we had grown to a staff of ten. And we were broke.

I felt miserable as I sat at my desk in tears one Friday afternoon trying to figure out how to make payroll. I was prayerful and trying to lead from my heart, but the decisions I was making as a young leader were not panning out the way I had envisioned. The staff size had to be reduced. I felt like a complete failure realizing other people were going to be hurt due to my poor decision-making. To reduce expenses, I was the first to leave and return to the private sector. My heart broke as I watched Tommy burdened with laying off person after person—people I had hired. The team shrank down to Jason, one sole employee. The challenges of an organization I started were now sitting squarely on the shoulders of one man.

"How did this happen?" I thought, as I reflected on things. I had courage, I had faith, but what I lacked was prudence. I had the zeal necessary to quit my job and work around the clock to achieve the Fraternus mission of "mentoring boys into virtuous Catholic men," but I didn't possess the prudence necessary to bridle and direct that passion. Having worked for the Boy Scouts, I knew *about* organizational structure, but I didn't have the experience of *building* an organization. There were holy men surrounding me, but my own pride kept me from leaning on their knowledge.

The "self-made" lie of my childhood blinded me into thinking I could and should handle it on my own. When I was a boy, I was the "man of the house" and lived by this inner vow that it was up to me to fix things—spiritually and physically. When something in our home would break, I would try to use tools I was unfamiliar with and often made things worse. It was as if I was in St. Joseph's workshop without St. Joseph. Now, I was in my twenties trying to manage Fraternus and the same thing had happened. I was living by the same lie, just functioning in a different workshop. Once again, the lack of fatherhood in my life resulted in a lack of prudence and wisdom about earthly and heavenly realities.

Through God's grace and the efforts of hundreds of volunteer men, the Fraternus organization survived that challenging time and is now thriving across the country. While I lacked prudence and resisted relying on help, the mission was reconciled by literally hundreds of fathers. I can see God the Father chuckling at me as I tried to accomplish this task on my own. Rendered helpless, these men stepped in. They filled the void. The volunteer men of Fraternus offered me a living example of St. Joseph. They have quietly and virtuously carried the mission of Fraternus forward, flanked by the help of many men. It is this brotherhood, and this example of St. Joseph, that makes the apostolate of Fraternus so powerful.

In my living room sits an old rocking chair that has been handed down to our family from my wife's great grandfather. It is the best chair in the house. It has a beautiful creaking sound when you rock. It is still so strong. I don't think it will ever break. You can't find a rocker like this in a store;

its character has taken decades to acquire. When I sit in that rocking chair, I contemplate St. Joseph. He was a carpenter, craftsman, and probably the best decision-maker that has ever lived—at least the best decision-maker conceived *with sin*.

When I sit in that rocker, I also think about my life. How many times should I have placed my trust in St. Joseph and asked him to be my surrogate father when I felt fatherless? How many times should I have asked him to help me make decisions when the path wasn't clear? Prudence is referred to as the guide of all other virtues. It literally means "seeing ahead." There are so many times in my life I wish I would have been able to see around the corner. However, my lack of experience and inability to trust my mentors limited my sight. These are times we are all invited to *ite ad Joseph* (go to Joseph) because prudence isn't constructed overnight. It is not something we can research on the internet and quickly acquire. I am still learning the way of St. Joseph and growing in this essential virtue.

I am now a father of seven children and am trying to go to Joseph as often as possible. Through my wealth management firm, I am constantly surrounded by men of prudence. Every day, I encounter pre-retirees and retirees who share their stories with me and provide examples of prudence. Their wisdom is a gift to me and perhaps one of the most valuable assets they pass on to their children. In my book *The Great Inheritance: 7 Steps to Leaving Behind More Than Your Money*,[4] I share how leaving behind *who you are* is more important than leaving behind *what you have*. Why? Because

---

[4]   Justin Biance, *The Great Inheritance; Seven Steps to Leaving Behind More Than Your Money* (Crescat Press, 2018).

a life journeying with the Lord creates a reservoir of wisdom. And that wisdom needs to be passed on. It needs to be shared with friends and coworkers, but most importantly, it needs to be passed on to the next generation. In the same way, St. Joseph shared his wisdom with Jesus.

The Holy Spirit has worked miracles in my life through many spiritual fathers both inside and outside of my day job. These men strengthened my understanding of St. Joseph's role as foster father. Not only were they examples of prudence, but they also taught me about honesty, perseverance, and healing. In deep gratitude to these spiritual fathers, I enjoy a reconciled relationship with my dad and an unbroken relationship with my children. Unlike the past missteps in my life, this healing was not accomplished through my own efforts. God can redeem what is lost and heal what has been broken. It is not something we can manufacture on our own; it isn't an area of our life where we can be "self-made." God is the Father of mercies; we simply must trust him throughout our journey and have the courage to receive it.

This past year I finished the attic of our home with my dad and my oldest son, Monroe. As we framed the walls of the room, I couldn't help but think about the father-son relationship between Jesus and St. Joseph. There were several moments when my dad was standing holding a stud, I was kneeling instructing Monroe, and Monroe was swinging the hammer. It was a beautiful picture of multigenerational connectedness. My dad was sharing what he knew; I was receiving this knowledge and sharing it with Monroe. Anytime the three of us are together working on a project, I think about St. Joseph's workshop.

Trying to be an example of St. Joseph—and God the Father—to my children and to those I lead is no small task. Life has changed a lot since I was a seven-year-old boy. I no longer go solo in any workshop I find myself in. Now, no matter the season or situation, I am dependent on the intercession of St. Joseph. I also rely on the wisdom of men in my personal and professional life. Whether it's the volunteer men of Fraternus, fellow fathers rearing children a few years ahead of me, or Legatus (a community of Catholic leaders), I am surrounded by men who live like St. Joseph. These men make prudence come alive. St. Joseph provides a vision of what it means to be a virtuous man. My prayer is that through following St. Joseph's example, we are all inspired to be a guide to the lost and a father to the fatherless.

St. Joseph, Most Prudent, *pray for us!*

Engaging the Message

1.	Pray with the following passage from Proverbs 13:20.

	"He who walks with wise men becomes wise,
	but the companion of fools will suffer harm."

	•	Read the Scripture passage once and become familiar with the text.
	•	Slowly read the passage a second time.
	•	Very, very slowly read the passage a third time, paying attention to the words and phrases that rest in your heart. What is God speaking to you through this passage?

2.	What qualities do you think a *wise* man must possess?

3. Do you know men who live out the virtue of prudence? What qualities do you admire in them?
4. Do you have a fatherly role model or brotherly friend to lean on? If not, what prevents you from seeking wisdom from other men?

Mobilizing the Mission

Be intentional about finding other men to walk with you on your journey. Join a Bible study, meet friends for a breakfast accountability group, or start a small group. Be an invitation for other men who may be too afraid to initiate.

Closing Prayer

Heavenly Father, I desire to live more fully the mission you have placed before me. I ask you to teach me how to rely on your wisdom and direction when I feel lost or directionless. I know that you are with me even when I can't see or hear you. You are always guiding me and encouraging me with your holy word. I desire to know you more. With your help, I want to grow in prudence and wisdom and eventually offer that hope to other men who are seeking it. Please give me insight and peace in the decisions I make today, tomorrow, and for the rest of my days. Thank you for showing me the way. Amen.

Justin Biance is a leader and entrepreneur in both nonprofit and corporate ventures. He is the cofounder of Fraternus, a Catholic mentoring apostolate for young men, and J. Biance Financial, a wealth management firm with offices in Florida and North Carolina. Justin is the author of two books, *Designed to Last* and *The Great Inheritance: 7 Steps to Leaving Behind More Than Your Money*. In addition to his work and writing, Justin's education is also a blend of faith and business. He holds two masters degrees, one in entrepreneurship from the University of Florida and a one in moral theology from Holy Apostles College and Seminary. Justin's greatest joy is spending time on his property in Western North Carolina with his wife, Angela, and their seven children.

CHAPTER 4

Joseph Most Courageous

"Be not afraid."[1]

—Pope St. John Paul II

Courage has many faces. Most of them are never seen. Not all heroes are found on the battlefield, the ballpark, or broadcast on TV. Most are found at home, at work, at church, in everyday life. Real acts of courage are momentary choices that ripple into a tsunamic grace that can change a landscape or a life.

Courage, or fortitude, is hailed as one of the four cardinal virtues of our faith. The *Catechism* explains that "fortitude is the moral virtue that ensures firmness in difficulties and constancy in the pursuit of the good. It strengthens the resolve to resist temptations and to overcome obstacles in the moral life. The virtue of fortitude enables one to conquer fear, even fear of death, and to face trials and persecutions."[2]

---

[1] Pope John Paul II, Homily, October 22, 1978, Vatican.va/content/john-paul-ii/en/homilies/1978/documents/hf_jp-ii_hom_19781022_inizio-pontificato.html.

[2] *Catechism of the Catholic Church* 1808.

Joseph was a courageous man. While he seemed to have lived a quiet and humble existence, it was anything but, considering he was called to father the Son of God. But he handled this call with prayerful resolve. At each crossroad, he chose to stand in the face of fear and be courageous in the moment. Joseph's life may seem extraordinary, but as you read Tom's story, you will see how each small, ordinary choice we make can have an enormous impact in the lives of others.

Be Bold

Dr. Tom Nelson

On a hot July morning in 2008, a momentary act of blind courage turned my world upside down. The fateful day started out in the usual frantic way. After necessary hospital rounds and rushed nursing home visits, I finally arrived at my medical practice a few minutes behind schedule. I hustled quickly from room to room to keep pace with a full docket of patients and a noon physician meeting that was tacked onto the end of my already tight schedule.

Between patients, my nurse handed me the chart of a seventy-two-year-old, white, unmarried, female named Joan. Joan had been a patient of mine since I began my practice in family medicine. My nurse indicated that there were several recent records ordered by Joan's cancer specialist to review in her chart. I had known that Joan had stage 4 lung cancer. Her tests revealed that her cancer was not responding to chemotherapy or radiation.

During my eighteen years as Joan's physician, I knew her

to be a very private person. Some might have even referred to her as a loner. Despite her tendency to keep to herself, Joan had a warm and welcoming smile that always brightened up the room. She had enjoyed the outdoors and exercise, evident by the well-manicured lawn of her beautifully landscaped home and the long walks she enjoyed with her dog, Punky. Joan also had a passion for sports. As a White Sox fan, she would constantly rib me about my Cubbies. She almost knew more about the Chicago Bears than their general manager. More than anything, Joan had a special place in her heart for youth and high school football. Living across from a youth football field, she would spend her weekends watching them practice and compete. She especially enjoyed reading about the success of local student athletes as they moved on to high school.

On that particular day, as she sat nervously across from me in my office, we spoke at length about the progression of her cancer. Together, we agreed that it was time to stop all treatment. As protocol, I began to inquire about out-of-town relatives and friends that could be present for her during this time and help facilitate and address social issues or anticipated needs.

Her response was a blank stare. She was embarrassed to admit that she had no one in her life to fill this intimate role. I had no idea that all her relatives were deceased. It seemed that her private lifestyle did not lend itself to having supportive friends. At this point, she worked up the clumsy courage to ask me a burning question. "I don't know how to say this, Dr. Tom. I need your help!"

As I sat in the presence of this frightened and humble

woman, my mouth became dry and my heart started racing. I arrived at the realization that Joan was asking me to become her caregiver. This personal request was totally outside of my comfort zone. In a moment of startling courage, I responded with, "Of course."

The rest of that day was a blur. Driving home, I pondered my *of course*. I was unclear if my response was a question or an affirmation. The more I thought of this unique encounter, I felt a tug at my heart that I could and should help. After seeking counsel from my wife, my father, and her attorney, I respectfully agreed to become her caregiver.

Over the next four months, my already chaotic life became insane. In addition to my duty as the managing partner of my medical practice, I was also the team physician and football coach at Nazareth Academy, a local Catholic high school run by the Sisters of St. Joseph. With all the responsibility I shouldered outside of the home, my wife and two children received what was left over at the end of these hectic days.

Nearly at the expense of my mental health, my *yes* to help Joan required me to make serious and much needed changes in my life. My *of course* was like an *I do*—a covenant relationship with an essential stranger. To top it off, Joan was not the easiest person to work with. In her fear and mistrust, she initially would not invite me into her home. Instead, she would hand me her laundry lists of errands through a partially opened door. To make matters more difficult, she was very particular about where I shopped for various items and where her bills needed to be paid. In spite of the initial awkward moments, a dear friendship was being cultivated.

In the beginning, our conversations centered around her

basic physical and medical needs. Little by little, the walls came down. After a few weeks, she became comfortable sharing her life story. She shared it with such enthusiasm that I felt as though she was doing so for the very first time. With all of our discussions about funeral arrangements and end of life issues, I felt the need to also attend to her spiritual needs. Faith was a hot topic. She would quickly change the subject any time I brought it up. She had admitted to being baptized Catholic but consistently rejected offers to receive the sacraments. What eventually surfaced were her feelings of unworthiness, shame, and guilt from falling away from the Faith after her father tragically died in a car accident.

Six weeks before she died, my heart grew restless watching Joan physically deteriorate. With great concern for the state of her soul, I reached out to a Catholic priest. Father Jim had been a longtime family friend, and he agreed to come and meet her. I confided in him that our appointment would have to be a surprise visit. He reassured me saying that "even if she is resistant to me being there, the worst thing that she can do is throw us out."

I distinctly remember the look on her face when we arrived. It was a potent mix of anger, fear, and betrayal, all directed at me. I couldn't look her in the eye. After pleading our case, Father Jim, in a matter-of-fact manner, sat down and started speaking to her like they were old friends. I sat next to Joan, hoping to comfort her and regain her trust. She gripped my hand with displeasure. As Father Jim spoke, it became increasingly clear that his words were those of Christ. Through him, Christ was speaking to Joan's nature as a beloved daughter and of God's unending love and mercy.

At some point in the conversation, she let go of my hand. With that subtle cue, I left them alone. This space made room for her to receive the holy and healing sacraments.

From that day forward, Joan was different. Her fear of death diminished. She was at peace. Our visits together were genuine and open. I felt like we shared more than a common friendship. Intellectually, I knew that as a physician, I had nothing to offer her. It was the healing power of the sacraments that allowed Joan to now receive God's love and support through me. It just felt so right. The Divine Physician and healer was showing me how he desired to work not just for her but through me.

On a crisp autumn evening, after coaching a football game, I quickly headed over to Joan's house to relieve my nurse and cover the next shift. By this time, Joan was in the care of hospice. My nurse reported that Joan had become unresponsive but appeared comfortable. However, not long after I arrived, her condition deteriorated. She began to transition into active death. Again, I found myself completely out of my comfort zone. I started to panic. You have to understand that doctors typically show up in the hospital after the patient has expired. We make the pronouncement or comfort the family. This experience with death was different. I was alone with a patient as she lay dying. Out of desperation, I called my wife, Anne. She offered me some much needed and grace-filled advice. "Get your rosary and pray. I will be here praying too."

As I held Joan's hand, her dog, Punky, stared at me from across the room. Praying those familiar and sacred words aloud provided me immense comfort. After the final *Glory*

Be, she breathed her last breath. In an instant, the room brightened. It felt like a completely different space. The peace I felt was indescribably powerful. Tears rolled down my cheeks. Punky, somehow aware her master was gone, quietly walked over and laid down next to me resting his head on my foot.

The ensuing months were difficult. After her burial, I left the cemetery with an image of me and the four gravediggers carrying Joan's casket to her final resting place, beside her parents. The whole experience was humbling beyond words. God seemed to be slowly revealing something to me. As I tried to discern what that was, my dear wife suggested spending time with our Lord in Eucharistic Adoration. This became a game changer.

My fast-paced life prevented me from seeing this spiritual opportunity. God the Son was waiting patiently for me to spend time with him so he could show me the abundant love of God the Father. He desired an intimate and ongoing friendship. This friendship evolved into a regular part of my prayer life. Here in this sacred place, I even brought the many demands involved with settling Joan's estate.

The humble and generous legacy of Joan Valenta lives on. Many lives have been influenced by her kindness. Funds were donated in her name to build a new football field and concession area at Nazareth Academy. The revenue from these facilities were then used to generate a perpetual scholarship fund serving the student athletes, who were so dear to her heart. The quote that I selected for the stadium's dedication plaque was from Deuteronomy 31:6: "Be strong and of good courage, do not fear or be in dread of them: for it is

the Lord your God who goes with you; he will not fail you
or forsake you."

Reflecting back on these words chosen for Joan's legacy, I
now realize this Scripture passage was for *me*. I was beginning to follow in the footsteps of a man I barely knew but
was slowly becoming acquainted with: St. Joseph. I pondered his courageous fatherhood as I knelt near a statue of
the Holy Family during these hours in the adoration chapel.
I was struck by Joseph's bravery, protecting the Christ child
and his mother Mary as they fled to Egypt.

Another bequest from Joan's estate was made to Woman's
Choice Services, a prolife organization where my wife vol-
unteered. For many years, Anne would share with me the
teachings of the Catholic Church regarding contraception.
However, her words seemed to fall on deaf ears. I must admit
that I was like most Catholics, marginally practicing my
faith. I was largely uneducated on the social teachings of the
church. Instead of going deeper into my faith, I remained
comfortable practicing medicine in the secular manner.
Instead of being rooted in my faith, I was deeply rooted in
our health care system. It was as if I was intellectually brain-
washed, unable to process incoming spiritual information.

By the grace of God, this was about to change. Anne and
I attended an event hosted by the Woman's Choice Services. As I listened to the speakers that night, their words
seemed directed to me. The first to speak was a physician.
He shared his story about a conviction to stop performing
tubal ligations within his OB-GYN practice. Next, a Catholic priest described the detrimental effects of oral contra-
ceptives on both marriages and the Church, as discussed in

the encyclical by Pope Paul VI, *Humanae Vitae*.[3] I felt these words penetrate my heart. I became acutely convicted of the need for change. I needed to integrate my faith into my medical practice and become a part of the solution. At the end of the evening, I felt gently lifted out of my seat. In front of the crowded room, I boldly declared my commitment to change. This rare moment of spontaneity was reminiscent of my "of course" response to Joan the year prior, another courageous declaration that ushered in deeper conversion.

In adoration the next morning, I felt as if the Lord was placing a sterile drape over my chest to begin a delicate heart surgery. I was so fearful of how I would stay committed to my promise to change. Much to my surprise, my physician colleagues and staff respected my decision. Aside from a few comments that I was interfering with the choice of the patients, I had confidence that the Lord would guide me. I also knew this would require prayer and fortitude.

My gynecological patients had mixed feelings. Initially, I would avoid the discussion with my strong-willed patients out of fear of rejection and judgment. However, as I persevered, I became more comfortable speaking about my faith and beliefs regarding contraception. Mercifully, I was able to do so in a supportive manner. I never wanted to impose guilt or shame to those who were using or requesting birth control. Most of the women had no problem seeing one of the other practitioners to address their contraceptive desires. Unfortunately, there was a fair number of women who did

---

[3]   Pope Paul VI, *Humanae Vitae*, Encyclical, July 25, 1968, http://www.vatican.va/content/paul-vi/en/encyclicals/documents/hf_p-vi_enc_25071968_humanae-vitae.html.

leave my care. They expressed not being able to understand how faith could interfere with their "health care choices." The grace from these struggles allowed for more open communication about human sexuality with all my patients. I was emboldened to speak more authentically with patients about their struggles with masturbation, promiscuity, sexually transmitted diseases, and unplanned pregnancy.

Soon, well-visits for those entering high school and college were not simply for completing check lists and forms. Candid discussions took place about abstinence, chastity, and cultivating healthy friendships. This included maintaining their relationship with God and understanding their identity as beloved children of God.

This grace-filled experience in my office soon helped transform my home. I was able to reorder my priorities. I resigned from my administrative duties in the office and modified my involvement at Nazareth High School. Even though both of my children had left for college, I was able to reclaim my vocation as father, leading like St. Joseph at home. A new awareness manifested during this time; I realized it was my responsibility to lead my wife and children to heaven. This time it was not simply knowledge of the head; rather, it was a deep understanding in my heart. I knew God the Father would continue to show me the way if I remained in his loving presence.

My time with Joan led me to the altar of Eucharistic adoration, imitating St. Joseph who would give himself frequently to adoring Jesus. One moment of courage led me to make space for my Savior, which in return ignited a holy boldness to courageously live out my vocation as husband, father, coach, and doctor.

Born out of my experience with Joan came a simple prayer I utter every morning on my knees.

Dear Lord, I surrender everything to your provision and your Mother's protection. Please allow me to live my life modeled after St. Joseph. Amen.

This personal prayer took on new meaning this past year after I consecrated myself to St. Joseph. Through this relationship with my spiritual father, I am inspired daily to live a life of courage.

St. Joseph, Most Courageous, *pray for us!*

Engaging the Message

1.   Pray with the following passage from Deuteronomy 31:6.

     "Be strong and of good courage, do not fear or be
     in dread of them: for it is the Lord your God who
     goes with you; he will not fail you or forsake you."

     •   Read the Scripture passage once and become familiar
         with the text.
     •   Slowly read the passage a second time.
     •   Very, very slowly read the passage a third time,
         paying attention to the words and phrases that rest
         in your heart. What is God speaking to you through
         this passage?

2.   What terrifies you?
3.   When you are faced with difficult choices, do you
     believe that *God is with you*?
4.   What acts of daily courage are you being called to
     make? List them here.

Mobilizing the Mission

Prayerfully discern an opportunity to walk outside of your comfort zone by honoring a request or helping someone in need this week.

Closing Prayer

Heavenly Father, thank you for revealing to me true courage. I ask for the grace to be aware of the places I have cowered from your will. Forgive me for the times I have chosen comfort over courage. Please grant me the grace to answer your daily call to walk out of my comfort zone and into your holy will. I long to be a man of virtue who stands in the face of challenges with fortitude and resolve. Reveal to me opportunities to be strong and courageous.

———————

Dr. Tom Nelson has been happily married to his wife, Anne, for thirty-six years, and they have been blessed with two children. He was the third born of nine children to Shirley and William Nelson. His father exemplified St. Joseph by the way he deeply loved his family and through his dedicated work as a family physician. It was the courageous heart of his father that inspired Dr. Tom to pursue a career in medicine.

After graduating from Chicago College of Osteopathic Medicine in 1987, Dr. Tom completed his family practice residency at LaGrange Memorial Hospital. He has been practicing medicine in Westchester for over thirty years, currently with AMITA Health Medical Group.

A major transformation of his faith occurred through the ministry of the John Paul II Healing Center in Tallahassee, beginning at a retreat in 2017. His eyes were opened to the (guidance of the) Divine Physician and Healer and the need to follow him more closely. Dr. Tom is now trained in prayer ministry and is active in the Joliet Diocese's Unbound ministry. He has been an instrument in the formation of Be Healed retreats also serving the diocese.

By integrating his faith and the healing power of prayer into his medical practice, he is now treating persons and families in their wholeness.

CHAPTER 5

Joseph Most Obedient

*"If you want to attain the fullness of joy, your
obedience must be the full obedience of love."[1]*

—Pope St. John Paul II

Joseph was obedient. In obedience, he took Mary as his
wife, freely loving a plan he did not conceive. In obedience, Joseph fled to Egypt, leaving behind everything he
knew to protect his wife and newborn son. In obedience,
Joseph lived a radically countercultural encounter with love.

Through Joseph's example of obedience, Jesus knew what
obedience looked like. Jesus humbled himself in obedience
to God by offering his life on the cross (see Phil 2:8). The
voice of a slave driver was not the voice that ordered Jesus up
the hill to Calvary. Love drove him to the cross.

Authentic obedience is rooted in an encounter of love.
Harsh and hypocritical voices will only drive us so far. When

1   Pope John Paul II, "Address of John Paul II to the Young People,"
     Speech, November 22, 1986, http://www.vatican.va/content/
     john-paul-ii/en/speeches/1986/november/documents/hf_jp-ii_
     spe_19861122_giovani-auckland-nuova-zelanda.html.

we learn and listen to the gentle voice of the Father, who freely beckons us to follow Jesus, we can truly offer ourselves in love.

The Church affirms that "the more one does what is good, the freer one becomes." In fact, she asserts, "There is not true freedom except in the service of what is good and just. The choice to disobey and do evil is an abuse of freedom and leads to the slavery of sin."[2]

Regardless of the destructive chorus of voices whispering lies about the goodness of God, we conquer the slavery of sin only in our obedient response to the loving Father.

As you read Father Burke's story, pay close attention to the voices he heard and how he responded. What motivated him to walk the path he walked? Think carefully about the voices you hear and the voices to which you respond. Are you able to hear God speaking? Do you know the will of your Father? Do you obey his voice?

Trust in the Father

Father Burke Masters

From the time I was seven years old, I dreamt of playing baseball on Wrigley Field. As I watched the Cubs from the crowded stands, I fell in love with the game and planned to one day become a major league player. This love of baseball teamed with a God-given talent to play was nurtured by my parents and cultivated by my work ethic. My plan was to make my dream a reality. I dedicated my life to this dream. I expected everyone, including God, to follow my plan.

---

[2]   *Catechism of the Catholic Church* 1733.

My parents sent me to Providence Catholic High School. We were not Catholic, but the school had a reputable baseball program and an excellent academic tradition. During my time at Providence, I grew as a player and I was *providentially* introduced to the Catholic Church. I was exposed to many aspects of the Faith, including priests, sisters, the Eucharist, and the beauty of a Catholic community.

During a school retreat in my junior year, my life was changed. I received the Eucharist *by accident* at Mass. A year later, a week before my high school graduation, I was baptized and confirmed into the Catholic Church and received my *second* Holy Communion. Around this same time, I received a scholarship to play baseball at Mississippi State University. As a new Catholic and graduate, I was ready to take the next step toward my major league dream.

At Mississippi State, I encountered my first disappointment. After performing well in the fall baseball season, I was informed by Coach Polk that I would be red-shirted in the spring. This was not part of my plan. When I arrived home that Thanksgiving, I informed my parents that I was not planning to return to school. As a player accustomed to starting, I couldn't imagine a season of sitting on the bench. My new plan was to transfer to a smaller school, near home, where I would start and play right away. My dad disagreed. In no uncertain terms, he told me that if I did not go back, I would be making the biggest mistake of my life.

To make a long story short, I reluctantly heeded my father's advice and returned to Mississippi. After redshirting my first year, I started the next four years. By the grace of God, I broke the Mississippi State and Southeastern

Conference records for hits in a career (the record has since been broken). In 1990, during my fifth and final year at Mississippi State, I had the game of my life. In the winner's-bracket game of the regional tournament against Florida State University, I went six for six and hit a grand slam in the top of the ninth inning to help our team advance and eventually make it to the College World Series. This was a dream come true. My grand slam was voted the top moment in Mississippi State sports history!

As I look back on my time in college, I cannot even think about what I almost missed. If I had not been redshirted in my first year, or if I had transferred, this dream would never have been realized. Obedience to my earthly father was key, trusting he knew what was best for me, even when I didn't know myself. Even after learning such a powerful lesson in obedience, trust was still hard to come by with my heavenly father.

When my plan seemed to derail again, I had to decide if I was able to trust God's plan. While I played briefly in the White Sox minor league system, I never made it to the major leagues. I was devastated. How could I ever reconcile my dreams with this deep unmet desire? How could God deny me this dream that I had worked so hard to accomplish? I simply couldn't understand why his plan did not line up with my own.

After working as an actuary for a short time, I decided that I would channel my desires into another career in baseball—a major league general manager. I received my master's degree in sports administration from Ohio University and started working for the Kane County Cougars, a Class A affiliate of the Florida Marlins in Geneva, IL. I felt at home working in baseball and quickly worked my way up the ladder. After four years, I received an offer to work in the front office with the Florida Marlins. Simultaneously, one of my college friends approached me with the possibility of joining his agency that represented several major league players. I was offered two dream jobs in baseball at the same time. Both were in line with my original plan. Both seemed to fulfill the desire. Yet, something told me that God might have other plans.

My girlfriend at the time had introduced me to Eucharistic adoration. Every Tuesday, we spent an hour in prayer. After years of avoiding silence, this time became my refuge. I suppose I had avoided silence because in the silence, we encounter God and confront ourselves. I was afraid of what God was going to ask of me. I was also afraid of facing my own broken places. However, as I pursued Jesus in weekly adoration, everything changed. That hour of prayer became the most peace-filled hour of my week. I began to long for this space to converse with God. In prayer, God spoke to me, repeating the same thing over and over. He was asking me to do something I wasn't sure was in line with *my* plans. He was asking me to become a priest.

Why not an agent or manager? Why a priest? It was too hard to reconcile. When I pictured becoming a priest, I imagined being lonely, bored, and poor. *Why would God call me to something that would make me miserable?*

I wrestled with God in prayer for many months. I did not want to be a priest. I still wanted to make a name for myself in the major leagues. I wanted to be rich and famous. I wasn't sure I trusted God. I felt safe relying solely on myself.

However, God persisted. Every time I stopped to pray, the idea of the priesthood surfaced. If that wasn't enough, random friends, family, and even complete strangers would tell me that I would make a great priest. I could not escape it.

As if God wasn't speaking loud enough, I heard a priest say that we ask the wrong question to young people. "We should not ask, 'What do *you* want to do when you grow up?' We should ask, 'What does *God* want you to do when you grow up?'" This caught my attention. Maybe I was asking the wrong question. If only I trusted his answer.

God met me in this place of doubt. After a powerful retreat, my spiritual life grew in leaps and bounds. My intellectual knowledge of God's love gave way to a deep knowledge of the heart. Finally, I believed that I was a beloved son of God. With this realization, my world changed. I began to trust. Trusting in God meant that he had a plan for my life that I could rest in. Because the voice of my Father was spoken in love, it was time to start listening. It was time to consider becoming a priest.

After continued discernment, the calling was confirmed. I entered seminary and never looked back. I have been a priest since 2002. I can confidently say it has been the most satisfying, fulfilling, and joyful season of my life. While my vocation requires sacrifices, my obedience to God has led to a deep peace.

My obedience also led to one of my greatest desires being fulfilled. In 2013, I received a call from Ray McKenna, founder and president of the Catholic Athletes for Christ.

Ray heard about my background as a baseball player and asked me if I'd be interested in becoming the Catholic chaplain for the Chicago Cubs. Can you believe it? Even though I was not exactly a Cubs fan at the time, I immediately accepted.

Amazingly, I began celebrating Mass for the players and employees at every home game at Wrigley Field and have now for seven years. During these Masses, I have gained a new perspective watching the players and the humble employees share the same sacrament and sitting side by side at Mass. I could finally see that we are all beloved children of God. God doesn't care how much money we make. He doesn't care about our status. He loves us, even those of us becoming self-professed Cub fans again.

As if being immersed in baseball again wasn't enough, God surprised me again. During a weekend at spring training in Arizona in 2016, I met with Cubs manager Joe Maddon. Unexpectedly, he asked if *I* wanted to practice with the team the following day. I couldn't believe it.

"Are you serious?"

"Absolutely. Come at 9:00 a.m. and we'll get you suited up with the guys."

I didn't sleep at all that night. The next morning, I anxiously made my way to the spring training complex. As I took the field with Kris Bryant, Anthony Rizzo, Miguel Montero, and others, I was in utter disbelief. During batting practice, I hung out in the outfield with Kyle Hendricks. As we comfortably conversed, tears began freely flowing down my face. My first thought was *Burke, there is no crying in baseball.* My second thought was *God, you are amazing!* It was as if God was saying to me, "Your dream was to play baseball in the major leagues, but you chose to live out my dream for you as a priest, and now you get to do both in the major leagues."

Later that year when the official season commenced, the team invited me onto Wrigley Field for batting practice. The first time I walked out with the team I immediately remembered seven-year-old Burke at his first game, dreaming of the day he would walk onto this field. In that moment, I realized that God's plan was bigger and better than my plan.

For too long, I trusted myself more than I trusted God. By his grace, I have learned that obedience to God and following his will is the key to living a life of joy and fulfillment, even if there are heavy crosses along the way. As our creator, God knows us and knows what will ultimately bring us joy. God has always had a bigger plan in mind for his children. No one, not even St. Joseph, could see how God's plan would turn out. St. Joseph's human example of trust teaches us to follow the will of God in our lives, even when what lies ahead seems uncertain or even impossible. Joseph is the model of obedience because he trusted that God's unusual plan was better than any plan his human mind could conceive or even dream of.

St. Joseph, Most Obedient, *pray for us!*

Engaging the Message

1.   Pray with the following passage from Jeremiah 29:11.

"For I know the plans I have for you, says the LORD, plans for welfare and not for evil, to give you a future and a hope."

- Read the Scripture passage once and become familiar with the text.
- Slowly read the passage a second time.
- Very, very slowly read the passage a third time, paying attention to the words and phrases that rest in your heart. What is God speaking to you through this passage?

2. How well did you obey your earthly father?
3. Do you trust the heavenly father loves you and has a fulfilling plan for your life?
4. Are you willing to obediently surrender your plan for God's plan?

Mobilizing the Mission

Find a time this week for Eucharistic Adoration. In the presence of Jesus, allow yourself fifteen to twenty minutes of real silence. Discover peace in the quiet. Ask God what he desires you to do. Allow God to speak. Then obey.

Closing Prayer

Heavenly Father, thank you for loving me even when I feel unlovable. While I do not always understand what you are doing, I desire to trust you more. Please forgive me for the times I disobeyed or disregarded my parents and others in authority and for disregarding your will for my life. I invite you into the places where I struggle with doubt and uncertainty and ask that you fill those places with your grace. I want to hear your voice and heed your call. I want to fulfill your mission. Here I am Lord. Send me. Amen.

Fr. Burke Masters was born and raised in Joliet, IL, the youngest of three boys. He converted to Catholicism at the age of eighteen just before going to Mississippi State University on a baseball scholarship. He played in the 1990 College World Series but did not make his dream of playing in the major leagues. He worked as an actuary for a short time, and then in the front office of the Kane County Cougars, a minor league baseball team. He felt the call to the priesthood and attended Mundelein Seminary and was ordained to the priesthood for the Diocese of Joliet on June 1, 2002. He served as the parochial vicar at St. Mary's Parish in West Chicago from 2002 to 2006. From 2006 to 2018, he served as the vocation director for the Diocese of Joliet. In August 2018, he became the secretary for Christian Formation and the director of the Office of Adult Formation for the Diocese of Joliet. He has served as the Catholic chaplain for the Chicago Cubs since 2013, including being a part of the momentous 2016 World Series Championship. He appears on Relevant Radio every Monday morning at 7:00 a.m. CST. He has recorded videos for the Knights of Columbus and writes a reflection on the daily Scriptures – www. frburke23.wordpress.com.

Chapter 6

Joseph Most Faithful

"St Joseph persevered in this mission with fidelity and love."[1]

—Pope St. John Paul II

Faithfulness is an inherent quality of God. He is faithful. Whenever he makes a promise, he keeps it, without exception. Scripture clearly asserts, "Know therefore that the LORD your God is God, the faithful God who keeps his covenant and steadfast love with those who love him and keep his commandments, to a thousand generations" (Dt 7:9). The *Catechism* supports this declaration, "The God of our faith . . . has made himself known as *'abounding in steadfast love and faithfulness'* (Ex 34:6, italics added)."[2] Evidence of his fidelity seamlessly stretches over salvation history. God, in making a covenant with his people, instituted an unbreakable bond, a solemn vow. God honored this vow.

---

[1]   Pope John Paul II, Homily, March 19, 2001, http://www.vatican.va/content/john-paul-ii/en/homilies/2001/documents/hf_jp-ii_hom_20010319_episcopal-ordination.html.

[2]   *Catechism of Catholic Church* 214.

Man did not. Yet, God, in his goodness, continued to pursue his people.

The marriage covenant is the closest human expression of God's covenant with us. The marriage between Joseph and Mary remains a prototype of fidelity. Their steadfast love also reveals God's faithfulness to each of us.

In the following story, Dr. Bob reflects on the virtue of faithfulness in his parent's marriage and in his own. As you read his testimony, take note of the places that his journey intersects with your own and how your upbringing has influenced your lens of fidelity.

Love Loyally

Dr. Bob Schuchts

I find it utterly amazing that God, who created the universe, entrusts his divine plans to mere human beings like you and me. Even when those human beings are exemplary in virtue, like the Blessed Virgin Mary and St. Joseph, it seems difficult to comprehend how any human person could be entrusted to represent God's faithfulness. Don't get me wrong. Mary and Joseph were personally chosen by the Father for this holy vocation. They are the most faithful human beings who ever lived, and the best possible parents for Jesus. But I wonder how they felt about the responsibility of demonstrating God's faithfulness to the Son of God.

Have you ever pondered the weight of responsibility Joseph might have experienced when he was called by the angel to be the husband of Mary? And then the added responsibility of being the human face of God's fatherly love and care for

Jesus? The Gospel writer Matthew tells us that he wanted to quietly divorce Mary, to whom he had already established a covenant (betrothal), possibly because it was more than he could comprehend (see Mt 1:18–25).[3] Yet even in this most challenging circumstance, Joseph remained faithful, first to God, then to Mary, and finally to Jesus.

As men, Joseph is our model in faithfulness. The order of our own faithfulness is equally important. Faithfulness begins with our covenant with God, then with our vocation, and finally in caring for the lives entrusted to our care. But few of us mortal men fare well under the kind of pressure Joseph faced. We can be faithful for a time, but our weaknesses rise to the surface when we are severely tested. I am speaking from personal experience, related to my father's unfaithfulness, as well as my own.

My dad was born in 1935, in Pittsburgh, PA. I have come to understand that my dad's faith in God was an important part of his life growing up. He attended Mass weekly, even though his parents did not go. From what I have learned, my dad was an exemplary athlete, at the top of his class as a student, and an admired leader at storied Mt. Lebanon High School. He and my mom met in ninth grade and began to date almost immediately.

---

[3] There are many different viewpoints among Church Fathers and modern exegetes regarding why Joseph considered divorcing Mary. They were betrothed, which was the beginning of their marriage covenant, but they were not yet living together. Did Joseph believe Mary was unfaithful to him and didn't want her stoned to death or humiliated? Or was he reluctant to live with her because he believed that the Holy Spirit was her spouse and he was not part of God's plan? The only thing we know for certain is that Joseph was faithful to God, to the Law, to Mary, and to Jesus.

His faithfulness faltered when he gave into sexual temptation in high school. Getting pregnant their senior year with my brother, Dave, my parents arranged an early wedding in the Church. Over the next twelve years, they would have six more children; I was second in line, born a year and a half after Dave. My memories of childhood are generally happy, mixed with a few traumatic experiences.[4] Faith was an important part of our daily lives. My parents sacrificed for us to go to Catholic schools, would pray with us each day, even coming into our rooms to bless us before going to sleep. They were actively involved in our lives in many ways.

I loved my dad and wanted to be just like him. He taught me to love God and his unfailing truth. He always encouraged me to pay attention while sitting next to him at Mass each week and then quizzed me on the readings and the homily after Mass on the way home from church. Overall, my dad was a faithful man, at least by all outward appearances. However, around the time I turned eleven, my dad's faithfulness wavered again. He would be gone after work and sometimes not come home at all after drinking too much at a bar. My parents began fighting. Later, we learned that my dad was being unfaithful to my mom. It devastated me to learn that the man I admired most was not living what he taught me. When I turned fourteen, he moved to another city, and we did not see or hear from him for two more years. My brother Dave eventually went looking for him and found that he had started another family. Once again, we were devastated by the news. At least this discovery afforded us the opportunity to be back in touch with my dad. This

---

[4]   See *Real Suffering* (TAN Books) for more details.

started what would become a long process of restoration and reconciliation.

As a young teenager, I had little awareness of the long-term impact my dad's unfaithfulness would have on my growth into adulthood. After struggling in school and sports for about a year, I too became a high achieving student, athlete, and leader in my high school. I also met my wife, Margie, in high school. Like my dad, I was unfaithful (to God, myself, and Margie) by being sexually involved with her before marriage. The one difference is that we did not get pregnant, because Margie was taking the pill (another unfaithfulness). During my junior year of college, we got married at Holy Family Catholic Church, professing our vows to love each other faithfully, in good times and bad, until death.

I admired the Holy Family. I was determined to model my life as a faithful husband and father after St. Joseph. But subconsciously, I lived in fear of being like my dad, who was unfaithful. My fears were rooted in my unhealed wounds and judgments toward him. I vowed I would not be unfaithful like he was. Furthermore, I resolved I would never divorce or hurt my wife and children the way he hurt me and our family. At the time, I didn't realize that these judgments and vows, based in pride and fear, would lead me to a moment of crisis in my own marriage.[5]

I thought I was being a good husband to my wife and a good father to our children, until these childhood wounds, vows, and judgements began to rear their ugly heads. I found myself withdrawing my heart from Margie and being

---

[5] For more on this see *Be Healed*, chapter 7, Anatomy of a Wound; and *Be Transformed*, 106–8.

less attentive to our children (who were around the age I was when my dad began to drift). Though I remained faithful to Margie sexually, my heart was moving away from her. I had no intention of divorcing her, but I was becoming emotionally disengaged—a kind of emotional divorce.

This realization of my emotional disengagement stirred tremendous anxiety within me. It also led me to seek God more intentionally, eventually realizing that he remained faithful even when I was not (see 2 Tm 2:13). During this time, a neighbor invited me to a Bible study, and on the very first day, I heard Jesus speak to my heart through a passage from the book of Revelation: "I know your works: you are neither cold nor hot. Would that you were cold or hot! So, because you are lukewarm, and neither cold nor hot, I will spew you out of my mouth" (Rv 2:19). This was not a comforting Bible verse. Rather, I understood that the Holy Spirit was showing me how my disengaged heart towards Margie was a mirror reflection of my lukewarm heart towards Jesus. In both cases, my halfheartedness was repulsive. This revelation threw me into a panic attack, which drove me to therapy for the first time. Until then, I had not realized that my halfheartedness was a protection against all the pain of my childhood and my lack of trust in God because of what happened. In therapy, I began addressing issues within my marriage, but the therapist was wise enough to see that the difficulties were more deeply rooted in my unresolved wounds with my father. For the first time in twenty years, I began to face and feel the sorrow of my dad's unfaithfulness and abandonment. This was a painful process that increased my need for God. In his loving providence, God the Father then led me to a Christian community with other men at my parish who were passionately living out their faith. For the first time in my life, I had real conversations with real men about real life and the real God—the ground of all reality.

Sadly, the distance with Margie was growing wider, as she did not share my renewed enthusiasm for faith; as a result, the wounds in our marriage remained unhealed. We tried marriage therapy, but it only made things worse when I tried to share with Margie how I felt. Things finally came to a head when we went to the beach together for a week of vacation, just the two of us. We hoped it would build intimacy, but instead it increased the hopelessness we each felt about our marriage. For the first time, we talked about divorce. I was finally confronting my worst fear and running up against my vow that I would not be like my father and hurt my wife and children how I had been hurt.

This was a decisive moment, in some ways like St. Joseph when he felt compelled to divorce Mary (though my heart was in a very different place than I imagine his was). I was at a crossroads, and thankfully, rather than rely on myself in this moment, I called out to God in desperate prayer. He answered me immediately and powerfully.

In the moment, I said to Margie, "I can't believe this is what God wants."

And she shocked me by saying, "No, this is not God's will."

In a moment, I felt free. I had avoided my worst fear, and Margie and I had come into agreement that we wanted to honor God's covenant more than we wanted to ease the pain of our circumstances.

After that, my heart began to change in significant ways, realizing that God was hearing and answering my prayers. Soon after, on a Christ Renews His Parish weekend, I experienced a powerful, life-changing encounter with the Holy Spirit, which filled my heart with joy. For the first time in my adult life, I knew the Father loved me intimately and passionately—and that his love was unlike anything I had experienced before. My younger brother Bart, also attending the retreat, experienced a powerful encounter with the Father's love too. Overcome with joy, we both embraced and cried in each other's arms. That weekend, I shed my first tears since my dad left, but these were tears of joy and release.

When I returned home after that retreat, I felt a renewed sense of hope and joy. When I saw Margie, I perceived her with new eyes and felt a deep love for her. I wrapped my arms around her, and we embraced in a way that we hadn't in a long time. I knew at that moment divorce was no longer an option, not because I feared hurting her and our children, but because I loved each of them and wanted to live for their good and to show them God's faithful love in a way that St. Joseph loved Mary and Jesus.

Space does not permit me to tell the rest of the story.[6] Suffice it to say, God remained faithful showing his merciful love and kindness to my entire family. Thirty years later when my wife Margie and my dad passed away (two weeks apart), my heart was at peace saying goodbye to each of them. My dad

---

[6]   *Be Healed, Be Devoted, Be Transformed* and *Real Suffering*. In those books, I share more of the process of healing and restoration that took place with Margie, with my dad, and with our extended family.

spent the last twenty-five years of his life back in the Church, faithfully married after receiving annulments. During that time, he remained active in ministry until he became sick in his eighties. After receiving last rites from a priest, he died in his wife's arms. At his funeral, all nine of his living children (from three families) and our mothers were all present. What could have been a very awkward situation was quite beautiful. We all sat together, and at the sign of peace, we exchanged God's love and peace with each other. God had brought about amazing healing throughout the years, and we could stand there celebrating *his* faithfulness.

The last months of Margie's life were sad for all of us but also incredibly beautiful because of God's intimate presence. He worked through her illness in amazing ways to bring us into deeper communion with him and each other. Each morning, I brought her the Eucharist, and we would pray together. We shared the joy of our love and faithfulness over the years while surrounded by the faithful love of our daughters, sons-in-law, grandchildren, friends, and extended family. After receiving last rites and an apostolic blessing, Margie died in my presence along with our daughters. Earlier that day, she said goodbye to our grandchildren, sons-in-law, and other family members. I was holding her hand and offering her back to God in those final hours, remembering the words from our vows, "till death do we part." Confident in God's merciful love and faithfulness, I believe we will all celebrate God's faithful love in heaven when our days on earth end. I shudder to think of how things might have turned out if God had not intervened in our marriage and family and kept us together during those challenging times. In a similar way,

I ponder what might have happened to Jesus and Mary if Joseph had not remained faithful to God's covenant. Would Jesus have been left unprotected and killed by Herod? Might Jesus have grown up without knowing a father?

There are so many people today left unprotected and unloved by a father. Unfaithfulness is evident everywhere. Is it any wonder people are losing faith in a faithful God? We need the example of St. Joseph's fidelity more than ever. Isn't it amazing that God entrusts mere human beings, like you and me, with the responsibility of demonstrating his faithful love? He trusts you. So be faithful as he is faithful, strengthened by his abiding grace.

St. Joseph, Most Faithful, *pray for us!*

Engaging the Message

1. Pray with the following passage from 2 Timothy 2:13.

   "If we are faithless, he remains faithful—for he cannot deny himself."

   - Read the Scripture passage once and become familiar with the text.
   - Slowly read the passage a second time.
   - Very, very slowly read the passage a third time, paying attention to the words and phrases that rest in your heart. What is God speaking to you through this passage?

2. Which men in your life have exemplified faithfulness?
3. In what ways have you been tempted to be unfaithful?
4. What can we learn from St. Joseph's example of faithfulness?

Mobilizing the Mission

Revisit and reflect on your baptismal, confirmation, and marriage/ordination vows. Make a commitment today to live them wholeheartedly.

Closing Prayer

Heavenly Father, thank you for your faithful and everlasting love for me. Grant me the courage to face the places in my life where I have been unfaithful to you and to those entrusted to my care. Forgive me for my infidelities, big and small. Give me a contrite and humble heart so that I may draw closer to your goodness and fidelity every time I am tempted to go astray. Strengthen me with your word and enkindle in me the fire of your Holy Spirit. In you may I become a living and breathing example of St. Joseph's faithfulness. Amen.

––––––––––––

Dr. Bob Schuchts, PhD, is the founder of the John Paul II Healing Center, where he and his team provide healing and equipping conferences for clergy, religious, married couples, men, women, and lay leaders. Bob (along with Jake Khym) has a popular podcast entitled *Restore the Glory* at www.restoretheglorypodcast.com.

Bob is the author of several books, including *Be Healed: Encountering the Powerful Love of Jesus in Your Life*; *Be Transformed: The Healing Power of the Sacraments*; *Be Devoted: Restoring Friendship, Passion and Communion in Your Marriage*; and *Real Suffering: Finding Hope and Healing in the Trials of Life*. His upcoming book is titled *Be Restored: Encountering Jesus' Merciful Love in Our Sexual Wounds*.

These books, along with recorded talks, conferences, and workbooks are available through www.jpiihealingcenter.org.

Bob and his wife, Margie, were married for forty-two years before she passed away in 2017. Bob has two grown daughters, who are married, and eight grandchildren, with many serving in the ministry at the John Paul II Healing Center.

CHAPTER 7

Mirror of Patience

*"To encounter the mystery takes patience, inner
purification, silence and waiting."[1]*

—Pope St. John Paul II

Scripture overflows with references to waiting. Wait for the Lord (see Ps 27). The Lord is good to those who wait (see Lam 3:25). Be patient (see Jas 5:7). Rejoice in our sufferings (see Rom 5:3). Our souls wait for the Lord (see Ps 33:20). Stay steadfast (see Jas 5:11). Wait in silence (see Ps 62:5). I will wait for the God of my salvation (see Mi 7:7).

Clearly, patience is paramount to the practice of our faith.

Joseph, given the title of Mirror of Patience, uniquely reflects this crucial aspect of faith. Joseph waited on God to reveal his divine plan. He waited for the humble stable to shelter his laboring wife. He waited for the wise men and for word on where to go next. He waited for two years in Egypt.

---

[1] John Paul II, General Audience, July 26, 2000, http://www.vatican.va/
content/john-paul-ii/en/audiences/2000/documents/hf_jp-ii_
aud_20000726.html.

He waited for three days before he found Jesus in the temple. As a carpenter, Joseph understood the importance of the process and the steadfast patience each project required. His humility allowed for the gradual progress of heroic virtue.

In a fast-paced, everything-at-your-fingertips, digital age, waiting has become a lost art. Culturally, we are averse to process and fixated on results. However, Joseph, through his example of embracing the process itself, can teach us that God's perfect will provides the provision, protection, and purification we each need on our journey of faith.

As you read Patrick's story, ask the Lord to show you the areas you have grown in patience and appreciated the process of waiting on the Lord. Inversely, ask the Lord to reveal places in your life that need purification in the practice of patience.

Give Everything to God

Patrick Lencioni

When I was a child, my mother used to regularly remind me that "patience is a virtue." My understanding of what she was telling me was pretty much limited to the idea that I shouldn't complain when I had to wait in line and that I needed to have more self-control. Knowing that I would grow up to be particularly impatient, and that I struggle with patience still, makes me wish I had better grasped the meaning of that statement.

Patience truly is a virtue, which means it can never simply be reduced to a matter of self-control. I needed then, and I need now, to rely on God for patience, and I need to understand that it is only through giving myself to him that I can practice the kind of patience worthy of the word *virtue*. Like any virtue, embracing patience means rejecting the world and the culture that the world presents.

I suppose my mom could have said to me when I fidgeted and complained at the doctor's office or in line at Disneyland or waiting for a sibling to get ready for school, "Patrick, let go of your attachment to immediate gratification and pleasure and control and achievement. Let God plan your days and your hours and your minutes, and accept whatever he gives you in the moment. That's what St. Joseph did, but he couldn't have done it without rejecting the world and submitting to God. You should do that too."

On the one hand, I probably would have rolled my eyes and wondered if my mom had gone crazy. On the other hand, it might have eventually made more sense. Such is the nature of virtue.

As a grown man with my own family, I now have to deal with my children who don't like to wait. I'm sure I've told them that patience is a virtue. But rather than give them the deeper lecture that I might have needed as a young man, there is something I have to do first: embrace patience in my own life. This is where rejecting the world becomes not merely a suggestion but a requirement.

As a businessman, patience is a tricky thing. Success is often a matter of finding a way to do things that the rest of the world has not. Innovation and strategic adeptness are, by their very nature, disruptive concepts, bringing about something new and better within an environment that isn't currently embracing those concepts.

Settling for the status quo, accepting the limitations that the industry or the market or the competitive landscape gives, is the antithesis of success. After thirty years of striving for success, it is no easier today to embrace patience than it was when I was a child sitting in the dreaded waiting room at the doctor's office, standing in line at Disneyland, or listening to my parish priest speak slowly and repetitively during a particularly long homily. Patience doesn't get easier as we get older; it simply becomes less praiseworthy.

The board of directors of a company is not going to remind a CEO that patience is a virtue. Niether is the vice president of sales at a software company, nor, for that matter, the coach of a professional football team. Patience is for losers, or so it seems in a world that defines a winner quite differently than God does.

And so the only way that I can overcome my impatience is to fully confront and acknowledge that the world today, and I suppose in all times, will not encourage me to be patient. It will tell me to seize the day, to cut through the red tape, to take control of my life. While those sayings are appropriate in the right context, the context in which the world uses them calls us to force our will onto our surroundings. In worldly terms, this is the very definition of success.

So, how am I, a man responsible for providing for my wife and family and leading my four sons into manhood, supposed to balance achievement and accomplishment with patience and submission? It's hard enough to do, let alone teach.

And that's where virtue comes into play, and the example of St. Joseph.

If patience is a virtue, and it is, it cannot be understood or embraced without seeing it in light of the chief virtue: humility. The other way to look at this is to understand that *impatience* does not stand alone as a vice but is a function of the chief sin: *pride*. As it turns out, my desire to cut the line and hurry the process and grab success by the throat, as much as it embodies impatience, is really grounded in pride. My pride. The bad kind of pride. The root of all sin.

This is the theoretical, intellectual, and philosophical breakthrough that gives me a fighting chance to embrace patience. If I attack impatience on my own, I will turn to self-control, which is just another form of pride. It's like overcoming gluttony by looking in the mirror every day; I will replace gluttony with vanity. If I try to prove to the world that I am patient—and that's what I thought I was supposed to do as a child, a young man, and even an older man—I will be discarding one of the "minor" vices for the major one.

The evil one must love this.

And this is where we need to understand, contemplate, and ask for the intercession of St. Joseph. You see, he was not simply a man of great self-control. He may have acted like one, but that was not his chief gift. He was not a man of singular wisdom, or kindness, or gentleness. Those may have been apparent in his actions and life. But before all else, Joseph was a man of deep humility. That is what made him such a good example of the other virtues. He knew God. He knew he was not God. And he knew that without God, he could do nothing. And with God, he could endure whatever the world threw at him.

Consider that St. Joseph was given the responsibility for protecting, teaching, and guiding the very Son of God. And yet he seems to blend into the background in the Gospels in spite of him finding a place for the birth of Jesus in Bethlehem, leading the escape of his family from Herod into Egypt, finding the lost child Jesus in Jerusalem, and providing for Mary and Jesus for years. Imagine the temptation that pride poses if we even shared a tiny fraction of that important responsibility! Yet Joseph quietly and humbly submitted himself to God.

Does that mean that St. Joseph didn't apply his skills and judgment, his sweat and energy, to the situations he encountered? Of course not. He must have embraced the spirit of St. Augustine's quote: "Pray as though everything depends on God, and work like everything depends on you."[2] Of course, the key to understanding that quote is understanding that all of our talents and decisions are gifts from God.

I don't know whether Joseph's carpentry business was successful. I often wonder the same thing about St. Paul and his tent-making. My guess is that they were extremely competent, extremely fair, and treated their clients with great respect, even love. Whether that translated to worldly success, financial gain, or reputational attention, I don't know. But even if it did, none of that would have settled into Joseph or Paul. If everything depends on God, then all benefits go to God. There is no room for keeping even a little of the credit. None.

And on the other side of the equation, if, after being

---

[2]　　This quote seems to be attributed to three saints (Augustine, Ignatius, and Benedict).

competent, fair, and loving, hardship comes, that too goes to God. We offer our worldly struggles, our financial challenges, and our reputational losses to him. And we have peace.

This is where I must go first, and where all who struggle with patience must go. We must shed every last attachment to ourselves. Our achievements are God's. Our struggles are God's. Our reputation is his. This is humility.

As I write this, I want to be clear that I have not mastered this patience thing. I fight the battle, not just every day, but multiple times during the day. The world is always waiting for a moment of weakness when I want my life to be about me. "Come on, just a little." And that is when pride wakes up, calls his friend impatience, and implores him, "Teach him the wrong definition of success. Make him feel foolish for submitting to God."

I am so thankful for being asked to write this chapter because it has forced me to sit and reflect on why patience has always been such a challenge for me. It reminds me that I cannot do patience on my own, or on its own. I must ask God to keep me aware of the connection between patience and humility. I must ask God to forgive me each time I embrace pride and impatience. And I must ask St. Joseph to intercede for me so that I may truly understand how he embodied true success, and to help me seek that kind as well, even if the world tells me I'm a fool for doing so.

God help me be a man of patience, by being a man of humility, by being a man who gives everything to you.

St. Joseph, Mirror of Patience, *pray for us!*

Engaging the Message

1. Pray with the following passage from Ephesians 4:1–2.

   "I therefore, a prisoner for the Lord, beg you to lead a life worthy of the calling to which you have been called, with all lowliness and meekness, with patience, forbearing one another in love."

   • Read the Scripture passage once and become familiar with the text.
   • Slowly read the passage a second time.
   • Very, very slowly read the passage a third time, paying attention to the words and phrases that rest in your heart. What is God speaking to you through this passage?

2. What situations reveal your lack of patience?
3. What did you learn from Patrick's story that would help you cultivate patience?
4. What areas of pride in your life stand as barrier to patience? Prayerfully ask the Lord to show you the root.

Mobilizing the Mission

This week, intentionally choose to wait on something that you would typically try to *make happen*. In the waiting, ask God to expose any areas of fear or pride that prevent you from seeing the circumstance as he sees it.

Closing Prayer

With praise and thanksgiving, I come to you, heavenly Father, asking for the grace to bear the people and circumstances in my life with love and patience. I ask for your forgiveness for putting myself above others and failing to see the opportunities I have missed while trying to get ahead. Show me the places of pride that prevent me from loving those around me. Teach me to embrace humility of heart and to renounce areas of self-sufficiency that prevent me from doing your holy will. I choose to put you first. Amen.

Patrick Lencioni is founder and president of The Table Group, a firm dedicated to providing organizations with ideas, products, and services that improve teamwork, clarity, and employee engagement. Lencioni's passion for organizations and the people who work in them is reflected in his writing, speaking, and executive consulting. He is the author of twelve best-selling books with nearly seven million copies sold. After eighteen years in print, his classic book *The Five Dysfunctions of a Team* remains a fixture on national bestseller lists. He is also the host of the popular business podcast *At The Table* with Patrick Lencioni. Pat's latest model, The Six Types of Working Genius, is designed to help people find joy and energy in their work. Prior to founding his firm, he worked as a corporate executive for Sybase, Oracle, and Bain & Company. Pat lives in the San Francisco Bay Area with his wife and four sons. Finally, he volunteers much of his time and focus to working for the Church through various Catholic organizations, including The Amazing Parish, an apostolate he recently cofounded, and released his first faith-based book for pastors entitled *The Better Pastor*.

Chapter 8

Lover of Poverty

*"Spiritual poverty entails the fruit of the
new heart, which God gives us."*[1]

—Pope St. John Paul II

"Blessed are the poor in spirit, for theirs is the kingdom of heaven" (Mt 5:3). For most of us, it is difficult to imagine poverty of any kind, much less as a blessing. While most Catholics tolerate mild mortifications, even the most devout Catholics will inevitably count the cost. No one chooses to lose everything. No one but Christ, that is. He gave his life so that we might have life and live it abundantly (see Jn 10:10). Wait a second. This seems like a contradiction. Blessed are the poor. Live abundantly. Which one is it?

It is both. We do not have to be financially poor to *know* poverty. We are all poor. Admitting our poverty is another story. Most of us work hard to compensate for

---

[1] Pope John Paul II, "Message of John Paul II for Lent 1998," September 9, 1997. http://www.vatican.va/content/john-paul-ii/en/messages/lent/documents/hf_jp-ii_mes_09091997_lent-1998.html.

our shortcomings by hiding behind our strengths. Like a clever comb-over, the bald spot remains. We all have our own patched-up places. No one is exempt. While material or financial are the most obvious types, poverty takes many different forms, such as poverty of time, intelligence, assistance, strength, health, resources, companionship, or community.

Paradoxically, this deficiency or weakness is the key that unlocks our yearning for a savior. This state of lacking connects us with our longing. Poverty (in whatever form) creates space for God to work. If we understand our spiritual deficits, we can begin to embrace our insufficiencies and inadequacies as the prime real estate where grace abides.

Only Jesus, our Savior, fulfills the ache and longings in our hearts. In holy confidence, "Jesus enjoins his disciples to prefer him to everything and everyone"[2] because he knew abundant life came only through him. This abundance was evident in the life of St. Joseph, who, bestowed with the title of Lover of Poverty, embraced this reality more than any earthly man did. St. Joseph, despite his lack of understanding, wealth, direction, or certainty, put Jesus and Mary first. As a result, he not only inherited the abundant kingdom but also carried it in his arms.

As your read Jake's story, pay attention to how he came to the realization of his own spiritual poverty. Ask the Holy Spirit to reveal places in your own life where you experience inadequacy and what the Lord may be saying in that place of poverty.

---

[2]   *Catechism of the Catholic Church* 2256.

Accept Every Weakness

Jake Khym

I've never been financially poor. Well, maybe once in college. After spending all my money eating out, I had to scrounge up $11.38 to pay off my overdrawn bank account by selling some CDs and using all the funds in my emergency savings account (coins in my truck's ashtray). Beyond that isolated incident, I have always had what I needed. Growing up in a middle-class family with hardworking parents who had good jobs, we had more than enough. My acquaintance with poverty came in a different form. Spiritual poverty. Through this awareness, I have learned a difficult and priceless lesson in growing in virtue.

Our culture lauds self-reliance. A man who can pull himself up by his bootstraps and keep fighting inspires us. I remember watching the *Rocky* movies as a kid. I was moved by Rocky Balboa's strength and determination. Who doesn't admire the self-made man? The man who grew up in the slums but with hard work and determination, overcame all odds. The cultural air we breathe fills us with the belief that real men don't need help.

For many of us, applauding spiritual poverty sounds a little ridiculous. Why would we accept our weakness? That seems like a recipe for disaster. Our weakness is what makes us, well, weak. That's never good, right? You never hear a guy with his friends watching the game (with a beer in his hand) tell the story of the time he rejoiced over not being able to fix the brakes on his truck. Who does that? Who loves weakness? Who loves poverty?

Enter St. Joseph, Lover of Poverty.

The Church is known for being counter-cultural, and the Litany of St. Joseph is no exception. St. Joseph apparently *loves* poverty. Before you shake your head and think, *I believe God is important and I want to go to heaven, but poverty is socially bad. And spiritual poverty? That's a pious thing for the saints, not for me.* Let's take a deeper look at what St. Joseph seems to love.

What kind of poverty are we talking about? And why would he love it? There's no way we are talking about rejoicing that a family of four can't make their rent payment. St. Joseph can't possibly love the idea of starving kids whose bodies tell the awful story of abject poverty. So what is it that St. Joseph loves? He loves when we realize that we are actually better men when we are strong enough to admit and accept that apart from Jesus, we can do nothing (see Jn 15:5). St. Joseph loves poverty because he knows a critically important truth that lies at the heart of the Christian message: *we can't save ourselves.*

St. Joseph learned this firsthand. Before CNN or Twitter, how did Joseph know that Herod sent out an army to track down and kill Jesus, as the Holy Family rested in Bethlehem (see Mt 2:13–14)? Joseph depended on God. Through the message of an angel, Joseph heeded the warning. Who knows what would have happened if Joseph relied on himself instead of God? St. Joseph knew that God is fiercely committed to the greatest good, our greatest good. In other words, St. Joseph loves our dependence on his son, our Savior. He loves that our poverty means we cannot rely on ourselves. Joseph knows we need someone who can do what we cannot.

I was never one to admit my weakness. In fact, my identity was deeply rooted in the belief that I had what it takes to be a man. I accomplished this through my own sheer grit and determination. At a young age, this belief took root. Sports were a major part of my childhood, and while playing a basketball game against my oldest brother, I found I had what it takes. I had been practicing for hours every day for a chance to beat him. My middle brother, Jason, was the referee. Having a referee was mostly for my protection. I may have been a little faster than my oldest brother, Joe, but he was much stronger. It was a good match that came down to a final shot (a boy's dream scenario). I had the ball. I made a move or two, took the shot, and . . . swish! I beat my oldest brother! I remember jumping around as I bathed in imaginary confetti falling from the sky. The crowd in attendance (the two neighborhood golden retrievers) stormed the court and celebrated with me. That day was amazing. It was a turning point for me. I remember saying to myself, "I can do anything!" Victory, hard work, and determination left me believing that success was up to me.

Roughly two decades after my basketball victory, I experienced many other powerful victories. I also experienced some agonizing defeats, especially as a result of my sexual addiction. Married with three young children, my wife and I barely survived this most difficult journey together.

Early exposure to pornography, coupled with some controlling wounds from my childhood, set me up for disaster. My holy ache for the feminine had become distorted.

I believed the lie that my hungry and hurting heart was never going to be satisfied. What was I to do? Take care of it myself. Satisfaction was up to me. A stark contrast to dependence and reliance on Jesus (see Jn 15:5).

If it seems like I am skipping over a few details, I am, but for good reason. Poverty was something revealed during my recovery. After facing and working through sexual addiction, I discovered something deeper than that nasty enslavement to selfish sexual pleasure: self-reliance.

This keen awareness arose while reading about the spiritual life in the *Rule for Hermits*.[3] I happened across a piercing quote. "Have the courage to let go of what is driving you." It was the question I asked myself next that haunted me.

What is driving me?

This question abruptly stopped me in my tracks. It was as if someone pulled the emergency brake in the car while speeding down the freeway. This question brought me underneath the hood of my life and caused me to look at what was really going on. These thoughts then became like an annoying warning light on the dashboard telling me something was wrong. Clearly, this question was not going away until the issue was addressed. As I stomached the question, trusting the inspiration, I began to unearth deeper dynamics in my heart. First, I had to admit that I was driven. Very driven. Overdriven. For so long, I considered my drive a virtue. I asked myself, "Isn't accomplishment and hard work a good thing?" But now, I was beginning to see with new eyes. My

---

3   Alberto E. Justo, Rule for Hermits (Santa Fe de la Vera Cruz: Centro de Estudios San Jerónimo, 1996), http://www.umilta.net/eremit.html.

heart was being pulled in two different directions. On one side was the deep belief that if I wanted anything good, it was up to me to go get it. And on the other side was Jesus saying, "Apart from me you can do nothing." I was stuck. Ironically, Jesus let me win this tug of war of the heart. He let me choose self-reliance, not because he was weak, but because he honored my freedom.

Not long after that, unaware of God's steady commitment to my healing, I came across a mind-blowing insight by St. Teresa of Avila in which she shared how self-reliance impeded her spiritual progress.[4] Similar to the *what was driving me* question, St. Teresa's reflections left me speechless. For most of my life, I have had this subtle, implicit belief that I had to merit the good life that Jesus offers. And while there might be a partial truth there, I took the merit thing really seriously and essentially believed, contrary to Jesus's words, "Apart from him, I had to do everything."

The problem wasn't my healthy urge to do *something*. The problem was I wanted to rely on my own strength and not rely on help. I was trying to prove myself because it was about myself. I started to see that my life was deeply self-centered. And despite how I wanted to twist the narrative, it was actually self-reliance (control) rooted in fear that was driving me. I simply couldn't get everything to work with more effort and increased skill. This realization was another serving of humble pie.

This theme of self-reliance started popping up in my everyday life and, more specifically, in my spiritual life. I

---

4   Teresa of Ávila, *The Collected Works of St. Teresa of Avila*, Vol. 1 (ICS Publications), p. 211.

realized that I couldn't do it all. I didn't have it together. I couldn't control every outcome. I was weak. I was poor. These realizations seriously irritated and alarmed me.

Since my identity was so deeply rooted in getting it right (whatever "it" is) and accomplishing things to impress people (or at least avoid their criticism), learning I am incapable was like being in front of a crowd and forgetting my lines. This feeling didn't just last for a moment or two; it occurred every day, multiple times a day. My inability, my poverty, was everywhere. I couldn't seem to respond right to my wife no matter how hard I tried. My work was mediocre at best. My prayer life was filled with the sound of my thumbs twiddling in an awkward silence waiting for God to show up.

After all the grumbling, fighting, whining, and wrestling with God, I slowly realized that I can't control everything. The truth is that in many areas of my life, I am in need. I am inadequate. I simply can't _____ (fill in the blank). This growing awareness was either going to be the death of me, my scarlet letter of shame, or my saving grace.

Providentially, I came across yet another compelling passage while reading the *Noon Day Devil*: "Holiness consists of such a state of poverty that at every moment one is obliged to ask everything of the Holy Spirit, one is dependent on him, awaiting his help, convinced that without his grace one can do nothing. This is the formation that God imposes on the souls with which he wills to work. He infuses docility in them through poverty."[5] This quote staggered me. Holiness,

---

5   R. Règue, Viens *Esprit Saint* (Venasque: Éditions du Carmel, 1998), 280 in Jean-Charles Nault, *The Noonday Devil: Acedia, the Unnamed Evil of Our Times* (Ignatius Press, Kindle Edition), Loc 1998.

the thing I really wanted and tried to earn, consists in such a state of *poverty* that at *every* moment, I have to ask *everything* from God. Wait, what? There it is again. I can't do it on my own. I was realizing even more that God was not going to let this theme go. He wanted my freedom more than I did. To my heart, it still felt like hearing "the earth is round" when I believed it was flat my whole life.

Finally, like a wrestler who knows he cannot escape an excruciating hold, I tapped out. I couldn't avoid the truth anymore. Achieving holiness is total dependence on God, not on me. Not just a bit of dependence here and there, but total dependence, like a car depends on a bridge to drive across the river. Dependent like a sailboat depends on the wind. Dependent like a baby is on his parents. Dependency is poverty. Let me stress that again; the dependence on God is the poverty. This dependency is holiness. This poverty must be what St. Joseph loves because he loves holiness, which is essentially loving and relying on God.

As I let this truth settle in my heart, I started to experience peace. I started to accept that if God is who he says he is, then that changes everything. If he's really trustworthy, then we can rely on him and our poverty and weakness isn't a deficit but a benefit. If God is good and really loves us, why worry? I simply can't make it better on my own anyway.

Poverty has received a bad rap. When we see it, accept it, and learn to love it, like St. Joseph, the power of poverty is unleashed. Whether our need is spiritual or material provision, we can stand with confidence that when we are weak, he is strong. God's power is made perfect in our weakness (see 2 Cor 12:9). After all, it is his power, in our poverty, that makes us rich in virtue.

St. Joseph, Lover of Poverty, *pray for us!*

Engaging the Message

1. Pray with the following passage from John 15:4–5.

   "Abide in me, and I in you. As the branch cannot bear fruit by itself, unless it abides in the vine, neither can you, unless you abide in me. I am the vine, you are the branches. He who abides in me, and I in him, he it is that bears much fruit, for apart from me you can do nothing."

   - Read the Scripture passage once and become familiar with the text.
   - Slowly read the passage a second time.
   - Very, very slowly read the passage a third time, paying attention to the words and phrases that rest in your heart. What is God speaking to you through this passage?

2. What drives you?
3. In what areas have you relied on yourself rather than on God?
4. Reflect on an experience when you relied on God to provide what you needed. What was the outcome?

Mobilizing the Mission

When you find yourself running into your own poverty this week and you are tempted to strive and push forward on your own grit and determination, stop what you are doing and admit your inadequacy aloud. Ask Jesus to fill this deficit with his grace. Allow yourself to rely on his abundance instead of dwelling on your lack.

Closing Prayer

Heavenly Father, I know that I can do nothing without you. You give me breath and life. Freely you have offered your life, holding nothing back from me in your sacrifice. Abide in the barren spaces of my life and water it with your abundant grace. Make my weaknesses and inadequacies become a dwelling place for your glory. Help me to be a lover of poverty like St. Joseph, trusting that in my lack there is room for your abundance. Amen.

Jake Khym has a master's degree in counseling psychology and a bachelor of arts in theology with a concentration in catechetics. Jake has worked in various settings for over twenty-five years, including adult faith formation, seminarian and priestly formation, diocesan evangelization, catechesis, RCIA, and retreat ministry. Jake has had a private counseling practice for fifteen years and also offers human and pastoral formation to the seminarians in the Archdiocese of Vancouver. Jake is cofounder and executive director of Life Restoration Ministries, a charity that seeks to awaken and restore disciples to Jesus, their authentic selves, and Kingdom living. Jake is a consultant to various dioceses and ministries across North America, offers a variety of workshops and retreats, and holds a large annual Men's Retreat in British Columbia, Canada. Jake also has two podcasts,

Way of the Heart, hosted with his friend Brett Powell for men desiring to live a full life, and *Restore the Glory*, hosted with Dr. Bob Schuchts, where they share their personal and professional experiences of healing and restoration. Jake also mentors male leaders on their journey of faith. He lives in Abbotsford, BC, Canada with his wife, Heather, and their three children. To contact or learn more about Jake go to www.liferestoration.ca.

CHAPTER 9

Model of Workmen

*"At the workbench where he plied his trade
together with Jesus, Joseph brought human work
closer to the mystery of the Redemption."*[1]

—Pope St. John Paul II

There is a certain satisfaction to a job well done. Most men thrive on confronting and completing difficult projects that produce tangible results. It is a deeply gratifying feeling no matter the job or profession. When this work offers a valuable service to the community and provision for life or family, work itself becomes a mission.

This mission of work is a mission for all humanity. The church affirms that "everyone should be able to draw from work the means of providing for his life and that of his family, and serving the human community."[2]

---

[1]   Pope John Paul II, *Redemptoris Custos*, Apostolic Exhortation, August 15, 1989, http://www.vatican.va/content/john-paul-ii/en/apost_exhortations/documents/hf_jp-ii_exh_15081989_redemptoris-custos.html.

[2]   *Catechism of the Catholic Church* 2428.

As central as work is to the human mission, all men struggle with it. Even the word *work* is now synonymous with toil and hardship. Whether the struggle is with finding the right work, wrestling with the nature of the work, or holding down work, each man, at one point or another, has felt the weight and burden of provision and purpose resting squarely on his shoulders.

However, the hardship in relation to work was not from God. After man rejected the gift of God in the garden, man was left to toil all the days of his life (see Gn 3:17). Toil is a universal masculine consequence of the fall.

That is until St. Joseph, the humble carpenter identified by his trade, elevated the mission of work for mankind. "Joseph brought human work closer to the mystery of the Redemption."[3] With Jesus at our side as we work, we can also take part in this mission. In our own workshops, offices, job sites, headquarters, parishes, and posts, our work can become a life-giving offering to our families, communities, and to the Body of Christ.

As you read Duane's testimony, allow the Holy Spirit to reveal places of struggle in your own work. Are you working with Jesus, or are you toiling alone? What places in your work does God desire to redeem through Joseph's example of work?

---

[3]   Pope John Paul II, *Redemptoris Custos*.

Pursue Balance

Duane Daunt

I never knew my dad. Like so many fatherless boys, I missed a few important life lessons along the way. Thankfully, my mom and grandparents filled in the deepest gaps. Collectively, they taught me a lesson that I quickly learned to live by: the value of hard work.

My grandparents were divorced and lived hundreds of miles apart, so I split my time between them. During the school year, I spent a lot of time with my grandmother in Miami. My *abuela* was an old-school Hispanic woman, both affectionate and demanding. She never shied away of laying out her expectations around the house or in the classroom. Education and hard work were in her DNA. Throughout my childhood, she passionately instilled these values in me.

My grandfather was a man of action. I had a front row seat to this action at the end of each school year when my mom would send me to Puerto Rico to spend the summer with my *abuelo*. I cherished the summers I spent with him. Despite my struggle to speak the Spanish language with the same ease as the other children, I loved my time in this tropical paradise. Most days, I followed my grandfather around and helped out on his farm. My grandfather was a hard-working man. He deeply valued a job well done and invested his whole self into every endeavor, and he expected the same of me. He would constantly model his relentless drive and attention to detail. He had great vision for the long-term outcome and would never settle for short-term satisfaction. He enjoyed the process of seeing his projects come to completion. As my primary male role model, I learned from him about what it means to be a man. The lessons were always about hard work and striving for excellence.

This double dose of work ethic was passed on to my mom. She was a daughter of divorced, immigrant parents and a single mom to two young kids. She worked her way through nursing school to ensure her kids had a better life and more opportunities. I have many vivid memories of her studying long hours and preparing for exams while working and balancing all of the endless demands of motherhood.

As much as I valued the lesson of hard work, another subtle and subversive message seeped in. I began to believe that in order to get anywhere, I needed to be totally self-reliant. It was only by hard work and willpower that I would succeed. It was up to me. With this message, I grew to be fiercely independent and focused on whatever I had to do in order to get ahead. It was neither safe nor efficient to rely on anyone else.

That independence and ambition served me well, for a time. I received a congressional appointment to the United States Air Force Academy in Colorado Springs, Colorado. During my time at the academy, I found a higher calling. Working with the men in my squadron, I learned valuable lessons of self-sacrifice and service to others. I also met lifelong friends, men who I consider brothers. These men became the groomsmen at my wedding and godfathers to my children. Throughout my time at the academy, I began to learn the importance of relying on others.

One of the greatest gifts I received in my life was meeting Carrie a few months before leaving for the academy. One thing that I noticed that was different about Carrie was her deep connection to her family and her faith. Her dad was the first man I met who talked and lived out his faith. While I had been baptized in the Catholic Church, I did not grow up going to Mass. While home visiting on breaks from school, I began to attend Mass with Carrie and her family. Because faith was important to her, it became important to me.

After graduation, I was stationed at my first base a few hours from Carrie's college. My roommate was a fellow academy graduate and best friend. He also had a deep faith and encouraged me to attend Mass with him weekly. It wasn't long after that when I asked my friend to become my sponsor in the Rite of Christian Initiation of Adults as I fully entered the Church.

During my year in RCIA, I had the opportunity to attend a father-son retreat with Carrie's dad, Bob. This retreat was centered on St. Joseph. This was the first time I became truly aware of St. Joseph (outside of my impression of him as an old man who was married to Mary). He was a saint I could truly identify with. I loved his title of workman. His life of service was inspiring to me. The retreat was also deeply healing. Attending the retreat and connecting with my future father-in-law, I gained a new understanding of spiritual fatherhood. Bob's faith and presence was what my fatherless heart needed.

Over the weekend, I also had the opportunity to experience adoration. This amazing encounter was the first time in my life that I was able to completely clear my mind and rest. For a man like me, whose internal motor is pursuit and perfection, this rest was new to me. Instead of *doing*, I learned that I could simply *be*.

Later that same year, Carrie and I were married in the Church. After five years of long-distance dating, it was such a joy to finally be together. While in grad school, we welcomed our oldest, Anna Kate, a few months before our next assignment to Wright Patterson Air Force Base in Dayton, Ohio. In Ohio, we welcomed not one but two wonderful baby boys to our family. Finding out about the third baby, we prayerfully discerned to separate from the Air Force and move closer to home to be surrounded by family. This was one of the most difficult decisions I have ever made. So much of my identity was wrapped up in being a man of honor and an officer in the United States Air Force. Moving to Tallahassee without a job, a home, or health insurance was a true leap of faith.

We were quickly blessed to find a job with a local firm that provided me with a good income and the ability to support our growing family. However, in the grind of the corporate world, I took my job as a provider to an extreme. I worked all the time to ensure that I was successful in my new role. All the while, I missed moments with my family. There were many late nights and weekends where I was more worried about my responsibilities at the office than I was about my responsibilities at home.

My pattern of being focused too much on work became a constant theme. In my head, I justified my need to work in order to support Carrie and our kids. It was my role and responsibility to ensure that I was a good provider. I was also living out a vow I had made that *my children would not go without* like I sometimes had to as a child. The singular focus on work continued to cause a deeper separation in our marriage. I was constantly stressed about work and the financial requirements associated with supporting a growing family that the cycle would continue: work more, stress more, work more, and so on and so forth.

After a few years and another baby, I had the opportunity to transition to another firm that offered better pay and more opportunities. I really enjoyed this position until the contract we were working under was cancelled and our entire office was either let go or moved to another location. At that time, we had been tossing around the idea of working full time in ministry, so when an opportunity presented itself, we jumped in headfirst.

Working for a small startup proved challenging on a number of fronts, especially from a financial standpoint. We spent every bit of savings we had accumulated and sold every investment that we had to our names. We were at rock bottom, and the stress of supporting a wife and four kids was overwhelming. During this period, I felt like an abject failure on all fronts. Carrie and I were arguing constantly, and we questioned our discernment, wondering if we had misunderstood the direction we were given. After several months, we began to look for another position in Tallahassee.

The job search was eventually a success, as I was able to find another job that provided an opportunity for us to get back onto our feet and earn enough income to offset the daily expenses. We were still way behind on bills, but we were blessed to have the chance to move forward, out of the rough patch we found ourselves in. After a couple of years, another opportunity presented itself with a larger firm working on a significant multi-year project for the state. The pay was very good and the benefits were a huge improvement. Finally, things were looking up and our prayers seemingly answered.

That is, until about six months into the project when I received notice that the state would not be moving forward with the project. Could this be happening *again*? I worked so hard and gave all of my time and yet continued to have issues with work. I began to look within the company internally and thought for sure that a company this large would have openings that could be filled by a current employee. As the months creeped by, nothing became available.

Over the course of those months, there were many sleepless nights when all of the self-doubt and questioning would creep in. Would I need to find a job in another city and sell our home that we loved so much? Would I be able to provide for my family? Was I not faithful enough? Was I not good enough? For a man who prided himself on being independent, I had no answers to these pressing questions.

During that time of introspection and self-questioning, I began to see things differently. The lull in work afforded me more time with my family. I felt a new freedom to simply *be*. I found it exhilarating to enjoy my family without the constant background pressure of work stress, unanswered emails, and phone calls. My perspective began to shift; it was no longer how much time I put in but where I put the time. I knew my family needed to be the most important factor. I was beginning to see that all of these challenges at work were not failures as much as opportunities. God was calling me to a shift of perspective and better balance in my life, and he was finally getting my attention.

This shift was a perfect transition to the next opportunity. With this new job and new commitment to tithing, God provided amply. Did this shift in perspective mean I could still be a dedicated employee striving to give my all for the company to succeed? Absolutely. I was not wired to function any other way. Were there times when work obligations required extra hours at night? Absolutely. The true shift that happened during that season was that *instead of this being the norm, it became the exception.* If I had a major deadline for a project or a procurement, I would make it up later by taking time off and spending some additional time with my family. They became my long-term project and most important investment.

I also realized that this approach to work is biblical. The work of creation was complete in six days, and on the seventh day, God rested. I am called to this same rhythm of work and rest—a rest where I can be free to just be. One of the biggest sacrifices (initially) for me has been our family's approach to Sunday. It used to be that I considered Sundays another opportunity to get work done around the house and get ahead for the week. After Mass, I would do yard work, painting, general fixes, and all of the other to-do list items that I needed to knock out before my real work began. Over time, I have been convicted of the true need to take a Sabbath rest, to be with my family and recharge. While there are occasional small chores required to keep our busy house afloat, like preparing dinner and cleaning up, the majority of the day is now spent focused on God and our family. We have a wonderful tradition of gathering for a huge family brunch every Sunday morning after Mass and dinner with family (and often friends) on Sunday evenings.

The balance of work and a large family is still a daily struggle. Even as I write this, I am cognizant of new places of pain that still exist in this arena. The temptation to overwork is one I constantly battle, especially as our two oldest kids have college tuitions. The reality of provision is always at the forefront of my mind. There are many days when I wonder how we are going to afford all that our family of ten needs. But the last twenty years have taught me that my family needs the love and presence of a father more than shoes, cars, or college. As head of our family, my primary *job* is to take care of our family, and this goes beyond just providing for their needs.

This past year, as life has slowed with the pandemic, I have had the opportunity to work on many projects with my kids. One project we completed together was building an oversized kitchen table to fit our growing family. Every time we sit at this table, I think of this precious time spent with my kids. I also think about St. Joseph and all the projects he built alongside Jesus. I am hardly the person St. Joseph is, but I take comfort in knowing he was a father and a worker just like me. He knew the struggle. He understood that his work is for the family and that his presence in that moment was the best provision.

St. Joseph, Model of Workmen, *pray for us!*

Engaging the Message

1. Pray with the following passage from Matthew 11:28.

    "Come to me, all who labor and are burdened,
    and I will give you rest."

    *   Read the Scripture passage once and become familiar
        with the text.
    *   Slowly read the passage a second time.
    *   Very, very slowly read the passage a third time,
        paying attention to the words and phrases that rest
        in your heart. What is God speaking to you through
        this passage?

2. In what areas are you burdened or struggle in
    relationship with work? Overwork? Sloth? Adequate
    provision? Purpose?
3. How do you maintain the balance of work and rest in
    your life?
4. What would it look like to invite Jesus into your
    workshop and make work a God-centered mission?

Mobilizing the Mission

Dedicate your workspace to St. Joseph. Every day, ask for
his intercession as you pour yourself into your mission. Follow your work week with a true Sabbath rest. Be intentional
about going to Mass and spending time with your family
and loved ones.

Closing Prayer

Jesus, I invite you into my workshop. I offer you my finances, my successes and my failures. I ask that you bless my work and my workspaces. Bless my productivity and bless my rest. Reveal new ways of meeting goals and new opportunities to pursue. Help me to order my minutes, hours, and days to your service. Give me a heart for the people you put in my path. Allow me to see the greater good over the immediate objective. Jesus, I ask that you lead and guide me in living out the true mission of work with you always at my side. Amen.

Duane Daunt is a graduate of the United States Air Force Academy and received his MBA from Florida State University. After serving his commitment in the Air Force, Duane began working in the private sector. Working first as a program manager, he eventually moved into business development for a large software company. His most important accomplishment was establishing Team Daunt in 1999, when he married his wife, Carrie. Together with their eight kids, they almost have enough *players* for a full-field soccer team. When he is not working or spending time with his family, Duane enjoys coaching soccer and woodworking in his (makeshift) workshop.

CHAPTER 10

Glory of Home Life &
Pillar of Families

"May the Holy Family, icon and model of every human family,
help each individual to walk in the spirit of Nazareth."[1]

—Pope St. John Paul II

G od is a communion of persons—the Father, the Son,
and the Holy Spirit—and he created man in his image
(see Gn 1:26). So it is in the family that we image God. This
eternal exchange of love is where the human mission begins.

God chose a family to be at the center of the incarnation (see Mt 1:18). Thus, God connected human families
with this divine mystery.[2] The Holy Family became the icon
for every human family.[3] And just as Jesus accompanied the
Holy Family in all the ordinary tasks of their vocation, the

---

[1]   Pope John Paul II, "Letter to Families," February 2, 1994, no.
        23, http://www.vatican.va/content/john-paul-ii/en/letters/1994/
        documents/hf_jp-ii_let_02021994_families.html.

[2]   *Catechism of the Catholic Church* 2205.

[3]   Pope John Paul II, "Letter to Families," no. 23.

Christian family is given the same mission of evangelization through love.[4] With Jesus at the center, Christian families live the faith through their particular state or vocation in life.

Joseph, in his role as head of the Holy Family, stepped into this mission by "making a total gift of himself, of his life and work; in having turned his human vocation to domestic love."[5] The same is true for our particular call. We are called to live the ordinary events of our daily lives with Christ's extraordinary love. The mission field is waiting.

As you read Chris's story, take note at what stirs in your heart. Pay attention to the parts of his story you relate to and the parts that challenge you. At the end of the chapter, you will have an opportunity to reflect on your own vocation and the mission God has given *you*.

Expand Your Circle

Chris Benzinger

Jesus. Mary. Joseph.

As a young boy at Blessed Sacrament School, the Benedictine sisters insisted that I write *J.M.J.* at the top of every paper. They called it a little prayer to the Holy Family. Even before I was aware, this *little prayer* had an enormous impact. For as long as I can remember, family has meant everything to me. My parents instilled this value from a very young age. We ate dinner as a family. We went to Mass as a family. We took

---

4   Ibid., no. 2.
5   Pope John Paul II, *Redemptoris Custos*, Apostolic Exhortation, August 15, 1989, no. 8, http://www.vatican.va/content/john-paul-ii/en/apost_exhortations/documents/hf_jp-ii_exh_15081989_redemptoris-custos.html.

summer vacations as family. We chased sunsets as a family. Family was central to my life. Yet when it became time to discern my vocation, the call to family life was still unclear.

The priesthood was also attractive to me. Growing up surrounded by holy and happy priests, I wondered if God had a similar call for my life. Priests were in and out of our house all the time. They would come over for dinner, play games, and just hang out like they were part of the family. Many told me that I would make a great priest. Their words were both encouraging and confusing. As much as I loved the priesthood, I couldn't imagine life apart from family.

At thirty years old, I was still discerning my vocation and found myself on a retreat in Arizona. My hope for the retreat was for God to give me direction in my vocation. After a talk by Bishop Sam Jacobs on personal holiness, I felt compelled to speak to him. With a fatherly gaze of tenderness, he told me he would be happy to talk to me. I proceeded to ask him how I was to know whether God was calling me to marriage or the priesthood. I shared with him that while I was open to the priesthood, family was deeply rooted in my heart.

As I finished sharing, he looked me in the eye and said, "Chris, do you love God?" I hesitated. I knew in that moment he was not looking for the right answer but for an honest answer.

He stepped closer and asked the question for a second time. "Chris, do you love God?" My hands were sweating and my heart was pounding, but nothing came out of my mouth. On the outside, my life looked very much like a person who loved God—full-time ministry, daily Mass, regular confession, and daily prayer. However, Bishop Sam was not asking if I did the things that someone who loves God was supposed to do; he was asking if I loved God with my whole heart.

After a few seconds, which felt like an eternity, he took another step closer, so close that I could feel his breath on my face as he asked the question a third time. "Chris, do you love God?"

"Yes! Yes, I love God!" I anxiously exclaimed.

Smiling, he said, "Good! If you choose to love God in this moment, then you love God. You see, God loves you! God is foremost concerned about your relationship with him."

Then holding his hand in front of my face, as if it was a check, he asked, "Have you ever written a check?"

I nodded.

"Chris, most of us are willing to write a check to God as long as we get to fill out the amount. If you really want to know what God wants for your life and even your vocation, write the check paid to the order of God. But leave the amount blank and then sign the check." Pausing, he continued, "Will you sign the check?"

In that moment, I finally realized I was focused on what I was going to give God. Bishop Sam was showing me that God wanted *me*, not what I can give him. God wanted my whole heart. He wanted my *yes* to his mission. Just as he wanted St. Joseph's wholehearted *yes* to his holy mission. Ultimately, this invitation was to an intimate relationship regardless of vocation. Once I stopped focusing on what I was going to give to God, I started entering into a deeper intimacy with him. It was then that God planted a peace in my heart and began to reveal my vocation.

With a new freedom to discern the priesthood and religious life, I spent time visiting religious communities and meeting with the vocations director in my diocese. It was on a particular visit with one of these orders, the Franciscan Friars of the Renewal, that the Holy Family showed up in the most unexpected way.

Prior to my visit, I got a phone call from a woman named Michelle at Franciscan University of Steubenville. Franciscan was starting a mission school in Mexico, and she was told to call me to get my input. In the conversation about family and missions, she talked about a Holy Family statue that she had seen at Holy Family Parish in Steubenville. She described the statue in detail.

Then on my visit with the friars, one of the brothers opened a gift that was given to them. The package contained a Holy Family statue. As soon as I saw it, I knew it had to be *the* statue my new friend had described in detail. The friar explained that due to their vow of poverty, they were not allowed to keep gifts. So, later that evening, I asked if I could have the statue to give to my friend. When I returned home, I immediately sent the statue to Michelle. At the time, I didn't think anything of it. I happened to receive the statue and innocently sent it to her. Her roommates at Steubenville had other ideas. "Who goes to visit a religious community and then sends a girl a Holy Family statue?"

Michelle and I downplayed the significance of the Holy Family statue and continued to talk, pray, and dream about the mission school. One Saturday in July, we took a full day retreat together to pray about the mission school. A priest had given us a few Scripture meditations that we used as a retreat format. For each Scripture passage, we spent an hour of individual prayer and then we came back together to share what we received. During the afternoon meditation, something shifted in my heart. I was no longer praying about the mission school but about being on mission with Michelle. I was confused. How would that work if I was a priest? I kept listening and then got the overwhelming sense that God had brought us together to be on mission *together* as husband and wife. I was both excited and nervous at the same time. How would Michelle respond when I told her about what I received in prayer? Was God revealing the same thing to her? As Michelle walked into the room, my heart raced. She looked different, or maybe I saw her differently in that moment. I did my best to contain my excitement. In true Michelle fashion, she didn't even wait to sit down to tell me that God had spoken to her in prayer as well. Unbelievably, God had revealed the same thing to her. In that moment, we knew that God was offering us both marriage *and* mission. We spent the rest of the evening reflecting on all the experiences of our short relationship that led us to this moment.

Days (yes, days!) later, I started searching for an engagement ring. Since we were going to live with the poor as missionaries, we wanted to keep the ring very simple. I found a thin, silver ring with "Jesus, Mary, Joseph" embossed on the surface. It was perfect—a constant prayer to be a holy missionary family inspired by the missionary family of Jesus, Mary, and Joseph. Two weeks later, on a retreat at Our Lady of Assumption Church on Pensacola Beach, the moment presented itself (with a little help from Michelle's mom and several eager friends). Sitting in the small Blessed Sacrament chapel, with the Holy Family statue sitting between the kneeler and the tabernacle and the "Jesus, Mary, Joseph" engagement ring in my pocket, we knelt down and prayed. Then I pulled out my guitar and sang her a song I wrote for our engagement. Tears began to flow. I reached my hand into my pocket for the ring, took her hands in mine, prayed a blessing over our relationship, professed my love for her and my desire to lay down my life for her as her husband, and asked her to marry me.

On the weekend of the feast of the Holy Family, only six months later, we were married in that same church. The entire weekend was a celebration of faith, family, and mission. Knowing that we were going on mission, we started a nonprofit called Trinity World Missions, and instead of gifts, we asked for donations to our missionary family. For the first three years of our married life, we lived exclusively on the support of our mission partners. Our wedding was a prayerful celebration of the sacrament of marriage and a beautiful send-off as a missionary family.

The very next day, Michelle and I flew to the Netherlands for a five-week missionary training at a retreat center in The Hague. Spending the first five weeks of our marriage with fifty other missionaries from around the world was such a gift. We were so encouraged by the other missionary families and the priests we met from Eastern Europe. Our original plan after training was to go live with the poor in Jamaica. However, during the mission training, the experienced missionary couples encouraged us first to be a part of a missionary community instead of in a leadership role. They told us that the enemy wants to destroy families and hates new marriages.

Toward the end of the training, we were praying for entire nations. Huge cutouts of nations from around the world were scattered all over the floor of the meeting space. Together, we walked around the room and prayed for each of these nations. It was at this prayer session that Michelle felt God's invitation to go to Austria. A few months later, after a short time back in the States, we were back on a plane to Europe to join the Austrian mission team. It was here that we experienced and learned the beauty of communal life. Two small families and a handful of singles cooked, cleaned, worshipped, studied, served, and led outreaches together.

Living in Europe, we decided to spend our first Christmas in Rome. Even though Michelle was almost eight months pregnant, she insisted on going. So we boarded an overnight train from Vienna. After Christmas Eve dinner at the American seminary, we made our way to St. Peter's for Midnight Mass. We were about seven rows back from the altar where Pope John Paul II celebrated Mass. Around one in the morning, when the celebration ended, we walked out into St. Peter's Square and looked for a taxi to take us back to the guesthouse. After thirty minutes of waiting, one of the locals saw us and told us that we were not going to find a taxi at this time of night on Christmas Eve. I felt terrible. There I was with a very pregnant wife two miles from our beds on a cold winter night in Rome with no way to get home. We started to walk, hoping that we would find a cab along the way. On the slow two-mile journey, we couldn't help but reflect on Joseph and Mary's Christmas Eve journey.

That following February, our first son was born in a small-town hospital in Mödling outside of Vienna. The attending midwife was skilled but could not communicate with us other than hand motions and the minimal German that I had picked up while living there. Fortunately, a doctor showed up who spoke a little English. While it was difficult to be all alone having our first baby far away from friends and family, it was a beautiful time to rely on God and on one another.

Our mission formation year in Austria culminated in the "Statmission" (City Mission) in Vienna. Cardinal Christoph Schönborn invited priests, religious, Catholic lay leaders, and missionaries from all over Europe to come together for a two-week mission in Vienna. Michelle and I (and four-month-old Noah) led a team of students and young adults from Franciscan University and Eastern Europeans studying at Franciscan's Austria campus.

Following the City Mission, we brought seven Austrian teens back to the States with us to experience a Steubenville Youth Conference and Life Teen Summer Camp at Covecrest. With the help of five young adults, Michelle and I led the Summer Camp with about one hundred teenagers. We had no idea at the time that one day thousands of teens would attend this camp each year.

After a couple weeks of leading camp, we moved to Mexico to serve as missionaries with a beautifully holy priest, Padre Santos Villegas. Our goal on that mission was to help him engage families, build strong marriages, and serve the poor. We learned that children make the best missionaries. Almost every afternoon, I put baby Noah in the stroller and walked him through the narrow streets lined with small houses on both sides. When women and children saw us coming, they called his name with delight, ran to us in the street, scooped him up out of the stroller, and took him into their homes to show the rest of the family. I followed them into their home and had some amazing conversations about family and faith, bringing Jesus right into their houses.

Soon after we arrived in Mexico, we found out we were pregnant with our second child. Michelle promised her mom that we would have our second baby in the States so she could be present. So we stayed until Michelle was seven months along and then flew home. The families of that little town became family to us. We were amazed at how many families came to say good-bye on the day of our departure. We came to them as missionaries, and we left as family. Leaving that community was one of the hardest days as family missionaries. It hurt to leave them, but we were reminded of our missionary training: "Whether you stay for a week, a month, or a year, love so much that it hurts to leave."

After the birth of our second son, Luke, our plan was to go back on foreign mission. We led missions to Mexico and Honduras with him in the first eight weeks of his life. He was a true missionary baby. As we were discerning our next mission, Randy Raus, the president of Life Teen, called and invited me to lunch. After catching up as friends, he asked if we were open to running the Life Teen Camp. He knew that I had dreamed of running a camp, but I was set on being a foreign missionary. I thanked him and declined. When I got home, I told Michelle about Randy's offer. She handed me the baby, gathered her prayer books, and left for adoration.

In her prayer, Michelle got the sense that we should seriously consider moving to the camp not only to run the camp for teens but to start a mission school that trained college students and young adults to be Catholic missionaries in the world. It became clear that God was inviting us to not only be a missionary family but to form hundreds of other missionaries. Covecrest was the perfect place to build an amazing Catholic camp for teens run by a prayerful missionary community.

God moves powerfully when a group of people are committed to daily personal and communal prayer, service to others, sharing the love of Jesus with guests, and caring intimately for one another in community. Hundreds of missionaries have been formed through Life Teen missions and serving the mission of Jesus Christ all over the nation and around the world.

While serving as camp and missions director at Covecrest, and having welcomed another son and a daughter into our family, Michelle's prayer prompted another revelation of God's expansive vision for our family. On January 12, 2010, a powerful earthquake decimated Haiti, killing over 200,000 people. Soon after we heard about the tragedy, Michelle's phone rang. It was her friend who had just gotten back from Haiti as a nurse on a medical mission. She told Michelle that she was flying back down to Haiti to set up a temporary clinic and asked if we could receive donations through our nonprofit to support her mission. We served as her state-side mission support and talked to her almost every day. She shared that Haiti looked like a war zone. Wounded people came to their medical tent from all directions, many of whom carried children who had lost their parents in the earthquake. One little boy was literally tossed into her arms as the woman begged her to find a family for the child. The nurse asked us if we could help her find a family for this baby boy and her pre-teen sister. The following Saturday, I walked through the side door of our house to Michelle, sitting on the couch, with her cell phone in her lap and tears running down her face. I saw her heart in those tears and knew that God had chosen us as the family for those two children.

After seven trips to Haiti and a lot of miracles over the next seventeen months, Olguine, David, and I walked through the revolving doors at the Atlanta airport. Our family of six grew to eight that day. As an adoptive dad, I know that family goes deeper than blood or biology. St. Joseph lived this truth about family life as he tenderly fathered Jesus as his own. My adopted kids are just as deep in my heart as my biological kids. Michelle articulated it best to our son David. "You were not born in my womb, you were born in my heart."

God's invitation to be a family is so much more than biological or even adopted family. It is ever expanding. Over our dining room table hangs a sign with a quote attributed to St. Teresa of Calcutta. It says, "The problem with our world is that we draw the circle of our family too small." This sign is not just a reminder but an invitation to take others into our hearts. After the adoption, God drew the circle of our family even bigger. In recent years, a few young adults have moved to our current hometown to be formed in "family" with us. We pray together. We share "big family" dinner every Sunday. We encourage one another in our human and spiritual growth. We do life together. Recently, Annie, one of the young adults, got engaged and moved to Chicago. At her "big family" dinner and send-off, we shared joyful memories that filled our eyes with tears and our hearts with love. As her spiritual family, we did not replace her family, we expanded her family, and she expanded ours. It hurt to send her off, but only because we loved her well. One of my favorite gifts I received from Annie was a Father's Day card that said "Happy Bonus-Dad Day" on the front. Inside the card, she defined Bonus-Dad as "a man besides your biological father who protects and defends you and loves you like you're his own, unconditionally, not because he has to but because he wants to."

All these years later I can see that just as the Holy Family prayer was scribbled on the top off all my papers at Blessed Sacrament School, family life was first inscribed in my heart. Family was his purposeful plan. Like St. Joseph, he only needed my *yes* to participate in his plan. And God's plans are always more glorious than our own.

St. Joseph, Glory of Home Life, *pray for us!*

St. Joseph, Pillar of Families, *pray for us!*

Engaging the Message

1.   Pray with the following passage from Ephesians 3:14–17.

   "I bow my knees before the Father, from whom every family in heaven and on earth is named, that according to the riches of his glory he may grant you to be strengthened with might through his Spirit in the inner man, and that Christ may dwell in your hearts through faith; that you, being rooted and grounded in love."

- Read the Scripture passage once and become familiar with the text.
- Slowly read the passage a second time.
- Very, very slowly read the passage a third time, paying attention to the words and phrases that rest in your heart. What is God speaking to you through this passage?

2. In what areas of your life are you reluctant to submit to the Father?
3. How would you draw your family circle?
4. Is there a place God is calling you to expand your circle? If so, what is holding you back?

Mobilizing the Mission

Make time this week to pray with those in your family or intimate circle. During this prayer time, impart a simple fatherly blessing of affirmation over each person in your circle. Ask God to show you others in your life that need to receive this blessing. Be intentional about blessing others through words of encouragement or generous deeds.

Closing Prayer

Heavenly Father, from whom every family in heaven and earth is named, I kneel before you, asking for your fatherly blessing over me as your beloved son. Strengthen me with your Holy Spirit and power. Dwell in my heart, root and ground me in your love. Bless my role within my family, helping me to love like St. Joseph. Allow me to engage in new places of strength as a son, brother, spouse, and father. Provide opportunities for me to grow in deep bonds of unity and to live a mission of love within my family and with my brothers and sisters in Christ. Amen.

––––––––––––

Chris Benzinger lives in Pensacola with his wife, Michelle, and their six children. Chris has been involved in Catholic ministry for the last twenty-five years. He has served in many capacities over the years, which include youth ministry, full-time foreign missionary, originator of Catholic missionaries at Life Teen Missions, and as a diocesan director of mission and evangelization in the Diocese of Pensacola-Tallahassee.

Together with his wife, Chris is also the creator of Greenhouse Collective, a ministry committed to creating safe and nurturing familial environments where people can heal, grow, and thrive. Most recently, Chris cofounded The Frassati Company, a consulting firm specializing in building strong leaders, healthy teams, and transformational cultures in both profit and nonprofit organizations.

CHAPTER 11

Guardian of Virgins

"Together with Mary, Joseph is the first
guardian of this divine mystery."[1]

—Pope St. John Paul II

Joseph was a guardian. But not just *any* guardian. He was the guardian of Jesus, innocence itself, and Mary, virgin of virgins.[2]

Can you imagine being responsible for the Savior of the universe, in addition to Mary, the purest creature ever created? Joseph must have been tempted to measure his role and question his capacity. Was he truly a worthy spouse to the Virgin Mary? Was he a *real* father to Jesus?

The Church recognizes that St. Joseph was both an authentic spouse and real father. Together with Mary, he shared in

---

[1] Pope John Paul II, *Redemptoris Custos*, Apostolic Exhortation, August 15, 1989, no. 5, http://www.vatican.va/content/john-paul-ii/en/apost_exhortations/documents/hf_jp-ii_exh_15081989_redemptoris-custos.html.

[2] See Oblates of St. Joseph, "For Purity," osjusa.org/prayers/for-purity/.

the same salvific event and was *the guardian of the same love, through the power of which the eternal Father "destined us to be his sons through Jesus Christ."*[3] Joseph was not a bystander at the Incarnation. He had an essential role.

John Paul II goes as far as to say that "Joseph is the father, his fatherhood is not one that derives from begetting offspring; but neither is it an 'apparent' or merely 'substitute' fatherhood. Rather, it is one that fully shares in authentic human fatherhood and the mission of a father in the family."[4]

In essence, St. Joseph exemplifies all the virtues of holy headship as he carries out his mission. At every intersection recorded in the Gospels, Joseph chooses to lay down his life as a guardian to those in his care. It is this act of service and love that reflects the heart of a loving father.

In the following story, Damon will share his revelations on his role as guardian over his family. As you read his testimony and hear about his struggles, ask yourself if there are places in your life where you question your worthiness to step into the role that God has been calling you to fulfill.

Protect the Innocent

Damon Owens

"We *will* love her and care for her as our own" was the reaffirmed promise my wife and I made to our daughter's birth mother, Karen, as I held Olivia for the first time in my arms in the tiny hospital room.

Karen had four children, worked full-time, and was a

3   Pope John Paul II, *Redemptoris Custos*, no. 1.
4   Ibid., no. 21.

full-time student when she discovered she was pregnant. Overwhelmed by the idea of another child, she made an appointment at the local abortion clinic. As she sat in the clinic filling out paperwork, she felt a strong conviction to get up and walk out. Passing by a group of people praying outside the clinic, she raced home to research crisis pregnancy resources.

In her own words, she never heard of a public adoption. She never thought people who wanted to raise someone else's child existed. After searching the internet, she reached out to Bethany Christian Services, a national adoption agency with a regional office. This is where she found our family profile, a profile that until that month had only been viewable within our home state of New Jersey. But after fifteen months of waiting for a placement, we decided to expand our reach to other states.

Studying our agency profile, Karen was one of the few mothers attracted to our big family. Although she was not Catholic, she sensed Olivia would be "blessed among women" as opposed to being "lost in a crowd" or somehow starved by limits of love and attention. Karen observed in our pictures and words both an ideal and a reality of family life where love is not divided but multiplied by each. Karen said that when she read our family profile, it was the first time she knew that someone could selflessly love this child.

Olivia joined our family as the seventh child and the seventh girl. She was our first experience with adoption. Initially, the jolting reality of fatherhood through adoption challenged what I thought I knew about myself as a Catholic, a husband, a father, and teacher of the Faith. I worried if

I would I be able to really love her like her sisters. I wondered if it would matter that I could not see Melanie or myself in her as I looked at her face, heard her voice, or watched her gestures. I pondered if I could father her with the same zeal, passion, and ease that her sisters drew out of me in their unique but familiar way. I questioned if she would really ever be *my* child. In the back of my mind, I wondered if forever there would be some unseen or unspoken asterisk after dad and daughter.

The whole birth experience was different from the word go. Our familiar nine months of Natural Family Planning charts, pregnancy tests, pre-natal visits, ultrasounds, birth coaching, and midwives was replaced by twenty-two months of paperwork, interviews, home inspections, dreams, doubts, waiting, fear, then a call to pack up the family and go to a city fourteen hours away *to wait*. Wait for another call.

I remember being vaguely aware of this being a St. Joseph moment for me. My study and teaching of Pope St. John Paul II's *Theology of the Body* gave me a new vocabulary and awareness to recognize many of these deeply relational realities with wonder and fascination. But I had not yet read *Redemptoris Custos* (Custodian of the Redeemer), John Paul's letter specifically on St. Joseph's true fatherhood to Jesus. I had not yet begun working through a *theology* of adoption: a supernatural reality signified by the icon of adoption. This whole experience was new, and I felt oddly unprepared.

Strangely, the uncertainty itself was familiar, and almost comforting. I had felt this feeling before throughout our fifteen years of marriage. I could recall crucial decisions of love and life where our "yes" became moments of grace and blessing far beyond the initial fear of the unknown. The first time we felt the terror of our *yes* was when we were dating and decided to stop having sex. This bold act of chastity opened us to a flood of graces leading us to the altar in 1993. The fear came back again as we embraced Natural Family Planning and trained, purified, and formed our sexually wounded hearts. This decision renewed wonder, fascination, awe, and reverence for God and our marriage. Then it showed up again before the birth of our first daughter, Naomi. This moment shattered and melted our fears of having and raising children. Our first prayers for Leah were uttered in our own *"Let's do it again!"* transfiguration moment before Naomi's umbilical cord was even cut. Our third daughter, Rachel, was conceived first as an ache that somebody was missing. Sitting in our first little New Jersey home with the chaos of two kids under the age of three, Melanie and I hesitated to share our longing with each other. I don't even remember who spoke first, but I do remember the joy of not having to explain or convince each other of such a crazy longing. Little did we know that the sense of somebody missing mixed with fear of the unknown would guide us like a Bethlehem star through the births of Therese, Collette, and Veronica, two miscarriages, and then the grace of adoption.

Looking into Olivia's eyes that first day, I felt the return of that uncertainty, doubt, and fear mixed with exhilaration. With a gaze, I wanted her to know *"You are safe. I am your father. Whoever you are, no matter how I may feel, I pledge my life to you. I will love you, guard you, protect you, honor you, defend you, provide for, and draw out the best you."*

In the moment, I marveled at how, only thirteen years earlier, such a pledge erupted from me at the first sight of Naomi. I didn't expect such a deep, guttural bonding at first sight, where my whole being, in an instant, was willing to forfeit all for the good of this *other*. It took years to get there with my beloved wife, Melanie. I was caught off guard when it happened in an instant with my first child.

My pledge to Olivia was no less sincere than with Naomi or Melanie, but different somehow—more sober, perhaps, without the ecstasy of a birth or a wedding. Perhaps it was the fragile nature of adoptive fatherhood. Karen could change her mind and listen to the pleading of her own mother, urging her to keep her baby. A birth father could show up at the last minute out of nowhere and challenge the adoption. One of the hundred signed papers could be out of order. Court agents and administrators from either state could end my fatherhood at any point before the whole thing was finalized. In the interim, we had no idea when we could name her, baptize her, and feed her as we saw fit. Then there remained the lingering fear that after all that, she still may not accept me as her father.

I was ashamed of my foreboding joy and muted ecstasy holding her at that moment, ashamed of my fear of taking her into my home. Even with her early doubts, Melanie seemed to slip right into amazing mother-mode without hesitation. But the question for me remained, "When will I feel like her father in the same way I felt with the others? *And what if I never do?*"

During the week of waiting to receive Olivia, Melanie and I found a local parish for daily Mass not far from the hotel. One morning, a friendly parishioner introduced himself and asked where we were from and what brought us into town. We told him about the adoption and our family, and I shared some of the foreboding joy of first-time adoption. As I anonymously shared some details of Karen's story, the parishioner stopped me, then called to several others to come hear the story. As I shared, I could see that the story somehow meant something to each of them. They held onto every word. Then a few began to weep. I could tell there was more to this story that I didn't know.

As the Lord lives, there was only one abortion clinic in that town. There was only one group that made a regular prayerful presence at that clinic. And the leader of that group was standing in front of me and motioning some of the other prayer warriors over to hear about a rescue they never knew occurred. As I heard them share about their faithful presence at the clinic, I was deeply consoled in that moment. I knew not to fear taking this child into my home. The Holy Spirit had been moving and weaving events beyond my vision to bring us to this moment. Like St. Joseph (see Mt 2), all of my hesitancy and fear diminished in one encounter of grace. For Joseph, it was a dream. For me, it was the encounter with these faithful prayer warriors. Every thin thread that connected decisions, events, and people was being woven together by God for *his* purpose. I began to see my fatherhood to Olivia as an irreplaceable part of that tapestry. God *called* and *gifted* me with her fatherhood. How dare I question that?

Truly, it didn't matter how I felt at the first moment or any particular moment along the way. The only thing that mattered was that I was obedient to the *munus*—the role, mission, vocation, high office, task, gift—that God had entrusted to me. *Munus* is a strange, but rich, Latin word that has opened up my mind and heart to my experience of fatherhood. This word was first presented to be me by Catholic scholar Dr. Janet Smith. She notes that the word *munus* is used in Scripture and in the writings of St. Thomas Aquinas to refer to both gifts that man consecrates to God and gifts and graces that man receives from God.[5] It is used nearly two hundred and fifty times in the documents of the Second Vatican Council, eighty-three times in *Familiaris Consortio* ("The Munus of the Christian Family in the Modern World"), and twenty-four times in *Humanae Vitae* ("The Most Serious Munus of the Transmission of Human Life").

Munus also helped Melanie and I understand marriage as the state of being of a mother (matrimony) and the state of being of a father (patrimony). Both matrimony and patrimony refer to both gifts that man consecrates to God and gifts and graces that man receives from God.

Throughout the chapters of this very book, we meditate on the many *munera* of St. Joseph named in the *Litany of St. Joseph*. Many of his titles and roles resonate with me as a man, son, father, and husband, but *Guardian of Virgins* holds special meaning for me as a father of seven daughters. It is too narrow to simply think of it meaning guarding their virginity, chastity, or even purity. That is an important part

---

5   "The Importance of the Concept of Munus to the Understanding of Humanae Vitae," Trust the Truth: A Symposium on the Twentieth Anniversary of the Encyclical Humanae Vitae (The Pope John Center, 1992).

of it, for sure. But the deeper meaning of such a *munus* is my active, life-long vocation to ensure the good of these children of God entrusted to my care.

How do I ensure their good? To father is to bring something into existence that cannot exist on its own, and to ensure its good, two crucial tasks of life and love. Fatherhood originates in God the Father precisely because everything comes from him, and he ensures the good of all creation. Human fatherhood, like mine, is a share in his Fatherhood to *co*-create (*pro*-create) and ensure the good of creation. Patrimony is a *munus* of both life *and* love.

Ultimately, what adoption has taught me is reverence for the *munus*. Regardless of their means of conception, every child is a gift, whom God entrusts to love back into perfect union with him.

Delayed but not denied, God granted me that outpouring of passion and joy for Olivia a few weeks after her birth. Shortly before her baptism, I remember gazing at her as an overwhelming grace erupted from deep within me. I could *see* her. Just as with her older sisters, I knew now *in my heart* that Olivia was my daughter and I was her father. No asterisks. No conditions. No reservations.

This was not the end of our story. God knew someone was still missing. A year later, Melanie called one Monday morning with an odd question. "Would we be open to watching a baby for a few days?"

Bethany Christian Services unexpectedly received a baby born on Saturday and the regular foster family was away on vacation. Since our home inspection was still valid from Olivia's adoption, they hoped we could care for him until the foster family returned. "Well, of course," I told Melanie, "but warn them we don't usually give babies back!"

It turns out, not *all* babies are girls! Nathan, born on my birthday, came to us that day and became my son. From the first moment I held this little baby boy, I *knew* he was my son. He was the answer to a prayer so deep in my heart that I dared not pray it aloud. Now Nathan, my son, is also "blessed among women" and under my guardianship with his sisters. Apparently, even such surprise adoptions are as much a part of God's plan as any other miracle in my marriage and family.

I thank God for the gift of my fatherhood. The good, the bad, and the ugly are all part of God moving, calling, and challenging me to continue becoming the son, husband, and father he created me to be. There is agony in this becoming, but a sweetness as well. The path is rarely clear or lighted. But God never promised that. He promised a lamp unto our feet. Perhaps that's why just doing that "next right thing" with peace and trust is one of my oldest spiritual challenges. My prayer is that the Lord will continue to guide me as he did the good St. Joseph. I thank God for entrusting me as ruler and *guardian* of my home. My prayer is that he grant me the grace to return his children to him as the saints he created them to be.

St. Joseph, Guardian of Virgins, *pray for us!*

Engaging the Message

1. Pray with the following passage from John 15:16.

   "You did not choose me, but I chose you and appointed you that you should go and bear fruit and that your fruit should abide; so that whatever you ask the Father in my name, he may give it to you."

- Read the Scripture passage once and become familiar with the text.
- Slowly read the passage a second time.
- Very, very slowly read the passage a third time, paying attention to the words and phrases that rest in your heart. What is God speaking to you through this passage?

2. What is the *munus* (mission) God has entrusted to you?
3. Do you ever entertain doubts about this calling? If so, name them.
4. Are you willing to sacrifice your own expectations or agendas for those you lead and guard? Why or why not?

Mobilizing the Mission

Thank God for the mission he has entrusted to you. Make a sacrifice this week for the benefit of another whom you have served, or continue to serve, as a guardian.

Closing Prayer

Heavenly Father, I give thanks for the places you have called me to lead and protect. I ask for your forgiveness for the times I have been either reluctant or domineering in my method. I ask for the grace to step into the places you have called me with confidence in you. I trust that you, God, will equip me in this calling and bless all those who are in my care or under my direction. Give me eyes to see others the way you see them. Anoint my mission and grant me the courage to offer my will for yours and to bear the fruit that only you have planted in my life. Guard my heart so that I may nobly guard and protect the hearts you have entrusted to my care. Amen.

Damon Owens, international speaker and evangelist, is executive director of Joyful Ever After (www.joyfuleverafter.org). The first executive director of the Theology of the Body Institute and chairman of the 2016 International Theology of the Body Congress, Damon founded Joyful Ever After as a nonprofit ministry dedicated to encouraging and educating couples to understand and live marriage and family life *together with joy* through St. John Paul II's *Theology of the Body.*

Host of the 2020 Catholic Marriage Summit, presenter at the 2019 Catholic Family Life Symposium, 2017 USCCB Convocation of Catholic Leaders, and 2015 World Meeting of Families, Damon keeps a full international speaking schedule at conferences, seminars, universities, high schools, seminaries, and parishes on the good news of marriage, sexuality, *Theology of the Body*, *Theology of the Family*, adoption, and NFP. In 2018, Pope Francis honored Damon with his Benemerenti Papal Medal in recognition for his work in support of marriage and family. Damon lives outside Philadelphia with his wife, Melanie, and their eight children.

CHAPTER 12

Comfort of the Troubled, Hope of the Sick, & Patron of the Dying

"Your sufferings, accepted and borne with unshakable faith, when joined to those of Christ take on extraordinary value for the life of the Church and the good of humanity."[1]

—Pope St. John Paul II

Jesus healed the sick. He raised the dead. He comforted the afflicted. Then he commissioned the apostles to do the same (see Mk 16:14–18). Healing is a central mission in the sacramental life of the Church. We are constantly called to be reconciled, strengthened, and renewed. Yet, illness and death remain. Suffering surrounds us. We cannot deny the reality of suffering and death that mark our existence this side of heaven. Even Jesus did not heal all the sick he encountered. How do we reconcile the reality of healing and suffering?

---

[1]   Pope John Paul II, "Message of the Holy Father John Paul II for the First Annual World Day of the Sick," October 21, 1992.

The *Catechism* sheds some light on Jesus's healing mission. "His healings were signs of the coming of the Kingdom of God. They announced a more radical healing: the victory over sin and death through his Passover. On the cross Christ took upon himself the whole weight of evil and took away the 'sin of the world' of which illness is only a consequence. By his passion and death on the cross, Christ has given a new meaning to suffering: it can henceforth configure us to him and unite us with his redemptive passion."[2]

This *new meaning of suffering* is in essence an opportunity for deeper union with Christ through our suffering. Our deeper union with Christ leads us to a more radical healing of eternal life in the kingdom of God. Healing is always drawing us closer to our redemption.

St. Joseph embraced this reality through his life of service and sacrifice for our redeemer, and now, after his earthly death, embraces his role as a powerful intercessor in heaven on our behalf. For this reason, he has been called the Comfort of the Afflicted, the Hope of the Sick, and Patron of a Happy Death.

As you read Deacon Tom's story, call upon St. Joseph to stir in your heart the places of affliction and illness in your own life that have drawn you closer to God. Then ask for his intercession as you examine the sorrows that have driven you further away from God's love. Ask the Holy Spirit to offer insight into the places God wants to meet you in your pain and suffering and the places he wants to heal your heart from the suffering you have borne.

---

[2]   *Catechism of the Catholic Church* 1505.

Carry Your Cross

Deacon Tom Thiltgen

Growing up on a farm in Iowa, I was acquainted with the revolving rhythm of the life cycle. The farm was always buzzing with new life. With the birth of young animals in the barn and the sprouting of seedlings in the field, joy and energy greeted me with each fresh season.

Farm life also exposed me to suffering. I watched animals born deformed. I saw livestock die at birth. I witnessed calves contract illnesses and never grow to maturity. Those encounters with death and suffering were troubling.

Yet, as I watched this cycle play itself out over and over again, I began to understand the certainty of this cycle. This was the way of life, the result of the Fall. Even with this perspective, death never lost its sting. I never grew numb to it. I just clearly recognized the order in it. Suffering and death were an inevitable part of life.

This perspective carried me into life outside of the farm. As a young child, I watched my grandfather, Tom, suffer with severe bipolar disorder and battle alcohol abuse, followed by institutionalization and separation from his family. I would often travel with my family to visit him at a large state-run mental health facility. I clearly remember meeting him in a large room with high ceilings, bars on the windows, and sparse furnishings. As I sat next to him and spoke to him, he hardly ever uttered a word. (I realized later this was because he was heavily sedated.) He seemed lonely and unloved. After each visit, I would lie awake and cry quietly in my room. *His suffering made no sense to me.*

I also watched my mother, Lizann, and my sister, Becky, suffer from cancer and die at the ages of fifty-seven and thirty-nine, respectively. The disease and treatments caused so much pain and suffering. They both underwent all types of medical procedures and medications with little or no hope for a cure or survival. Again, as an adult man, the same feeling would overcome me. *Their suffering made no sense to me.*

I journeyed with Mary, my beautiful bride of forty-five years, as she battled several forms of cancer over a fifteen-year period. The last two years were vicious as her cancer returned and settled first in her bones, then in her brain, and finally moving to her lungs. The love of my life, the mother of my children, and my earthly role model of sacrifice and love was brutally battered over and over again with radiation, chemo treatments, multiple brain surgeries, and medications that left her in a state of dysfunction. *Mary's suffering made no sense to me.*

After my ordination to the permanent diaconate, I began work as a part-time chaplain at a local hospital and as the celebrant of funeral services at local funeral homes. After listening to the stories of the sick, bereaved, and suffering, and watching them struggle with faith, I would ache for them and sometimes go home and weep. I felt as if I could do nothing to help alleviate or diminish their pain. I would begin to wonder again why there was so much sorrow. *The suffering made no sense to me.*

Trying to make sense of suffering, I would question God. How could a good God, who loves us so much, allow such awful suffering to be endured by his children? It was troubling to me that the God that I honored and praised sometimes seemed so distant and unavailable when he was needed most.

Ultimately, it was in prayer and meditation *with* God that helped me to perceive pain and suffering in a new light. Contemplating the suffering of my grandfather, my mother, my sister, my wife, and the hurting people I served in ministry, I realized that suffering is a mystery—a mystery from not just a purely physical perspective but an emotional and spiritual perspective as well. It is in this mystery that we somehow find that God is present even in the pain. The privilege of journeying with someone in their pain and suffering is sacred. In those moments, I encounter the mystery and an opportunity for faith. It is a mystery in that it is beyond my own ability to make sense of the suffering. It requires faith in that it directs me to trust that there is a purpose in God's master plan.

This posture of trust is similar to the faith St. Joseph had as he cared for Mary and Jesus. I, too, am invited to be patient, present, and prayerful in the middle of the mystery. As I practiced these three virtues, I began to feel more united to the will of the Father. In patience, I learned to allow circumstances to unfold before reacting to them. I also accepted that being present in the moment made every moment more fulfilling. Lastly, I learned that being prayerful in the suffering was remarkably comforting. Once I gave myself permission to be *patient* with the circumstance, *present* in the moment, and *prayerful* with the pain, the suffering with illness and death were easier to understand and accept.

Patience is one of the most difficult virtues to perfect. Humans move at an unnerving pace, and we often feel that if we don't keep up, we will be left behind. Yet, I have found that with patience, I give consent to experience the beautiful nuances that are typically missed. While difficult to practice, I have found patience to be a gift of grace.

One of the many ministries that I fulfill in my role as deacon is working with one of the local funeral homes presiding at services and interments when the Catholic family does not want a Mass or doesn't have a relationship with a local parish. Often, the deceased is someone I prayed with at the hospital as chaplain, which leads the family of the deceased to ask me to lead the service for their burial. It is not uncommon for the family to be inactive in the practice of their faith. When I lead the services, their confusion and unfamiliarity is quite apparent. I have observed that younger generations have little exposure with prayer, the Church, or even Jesus. In these services, I make certain to share the powerful message of God's love and mercy. I am saddened when I sense that the message seems lost or meaningless to those present. My heart aches for the bereaved family members because I know how much God loves them and how much God wants to be close to them, especially in their suffering. In these moments, I am learning to die to my will and timing and patiently wait for God to encounter them. I imagine this may be how St. Joseph felt as he observed people ignore and dismiss his adopted son. I, too, am called to trust the Holy Spirit in these moments. Trusting that the words that come from my mouth are what God wants them to hear. It is a challenge not to become discouraged. However, in patience, I choose to believe that these seeds will bear fruit when the time is ripe.

On occasion, someone will stop to talk with me after the service and ask a question about Jesus, faith, Catholicism, or eternal life. In those rare moments, my heart soars because a seed of faith is beginning to sprout before my eyes. Most gratifying are those occasions when I witness a renewed hunger for Mass from fallen-away Catholics. Encountering those individuals in the pews, I rejoice. I know God has been patiently waiting for them to come home.

Presence unfolds in concert with patience. When I give myself permission to be in the moment and soak it all in, I become enthralled with what is right in front of me. Refusing to dwell in past pain or future dread is truly freeing in the moment. So often I feel that I should be saying or doing something. But in just being quietly present, I am honoring and respecting the beauty of this beloved child of God. In those moments of presence, I can see life and relationships in a clear and unfiltered light.

As I had mentioned earlier, my work as a hospital chaplain places me in the midst of many people who are sick, suffering, and dying. My presence was often the most powerful and soothing thing that I could offer. Listening to their stories and empathizing with their struggles was like a soothing balm to them. There were times that I would feel lost and very alone and vulnerable as I listened to their stories. I would find myself thinking of situations in my own life that hadn't worked out. I felt their pain and suffering and hurt and betrayal and abandonment. Yet, there were the other times that I would delight in their happiness and joy as they relived those beautiful moments that brought them peace.

Being present with people in their last moments is very

sacred to me. I have been blessed to be with many people as they took their last breath. It is truly a holy and sacred time and one in which I have always felt divine presence and a sense of calm and peace.

I was blessed to be able to be with my wife, Mary, as she died in the hospital. I was alone with her and holding her in my arms as she was welcomed by the bright light that so many who have had near-death experiences share. There was a profound and unexplained stillness that entered the hospital room and an aura of peacefulness. As I gazed upon Mary in that last moment, I saw the most gentle and peaceful smile spread across her face.

I know that losing a spouse, child, sibling, or parent is one of the most difficult and painful experiences you will encounter. Yet, I also know that if you have faith in God and believe in the resurrection and eternal life, death can be a time of joy and rejoicing. I experienced this as my beautiful bride passed. She left years of suffering, sickness, and pain for a place of warmth, peace, love, and perfection. This is truly the greatest grace of presence.

Imagine how much more meaningful prayer is when we are truly patient and fully present. Prayer becomes pure, honest, and free. The boundaries that we place around our prayer dissolves into a sincere heartfelt encounter with God. I experienced this firsthand in my ministry at the hospital. There were times when I would stand silently in a patient's room for hours saying nothing, praying quietly, and being present to them. I was fully aware that exhibiting patience and being present while praying for them was comforting to both of us.

It was in prayer that the Lord reminded me of a Scripture passage a family had chosen for a funeral service: "The souls of the righteous are in the hand of God, and no torment will ever touch them. . . . Having been disciplined a little, they will receive great good, because God tested them and found them worthy of himself" (Ws 3:1, 5). Through this Scripture passage, the Holy Spirit provided me with insight into some of the suffering and sickness we endure in our lives. The times we are "chastised a little" are those times when we experience the process of purification before God. I realized that everyone handles this in their own way. This assurance is given to us directly from Jesus through prayer and in Scripture. He shares in John 14, "Let not your hearts be troubled; believe in God, believe also in me. . . . I go to prepare a place for you . . . that where I am you may be also" (vv. 1, 2, 3). Jesus comforts us and tells us to not be worried since he has a place of peace and joy awaiting us in heaven.

Our Lord goes on to tell us, "I am the way, and the truth, and the life; no one comes to the Father, but by me" (Jn 14:6). It is through our baptism, and our belief in Jesus as the Savior and through living a life in service to God, that we inherit eternal life. It is through prayer that we cultivate faith. If we have this faith and believe this, then death is nothing more than the next step we each take toward life eternal.

So, Mary's death, albeit a devastating event for me and my children and grandchildren, was a celebration of our Catholic faith and of the comfort in knowing that she was no longer suffering pain but on her way to eternal peace and joy in a place Jesus had prepared for her.

Prayer gives us a strong and resilient faith in God, Jesus

Christ, and the Holy Spirit to comfort and to guide us on our journeys from this earthly life to the life eternal, in the "place prepared for you" in heaven. I imagine St. Joseph offering in prayer the challenges in his life for the fulfillment of the kingdom of God brought about through the life and death of Jesus. I, too, am drawn to this life of prayer.

Through the grace of patience, presence, and prayer, I now have an acute awareness of God's merciful love for each of us. In this season, I see the cycle of life through a new lens. Death does not have the final word. Another new season awaits us. Eternity.

St. Joseph, Comfort of the Troubled, *pray for us!*

St. Joseph, Hope of the Sick, *pray for us!*

St. Joseph, Patron of the Dying, *pray for us!*

Engaging the Message

1. Pray with the following passage from Wisdom 3:1–5.

> "But the souls of the righteous are in the hand of God,
>
> and no torment will ever touch them.
>
> In the eyes of the foolish they seemed to have died,
>
> and their departure was thought to be an affliction,
>
> and their going from us to be their destruction;
>
> but they are at peace.
>
> For though in the sight of men they were punished,
>
> their hope is full of immortality.
>
> Having been disciplined a little, they will receive great good,
>
> because God tested them and found them worthy of himself."

- Read the Scripture passage once and become familiar with the text.
- Slowly read the passage a second time.
- Very, very slowly read the passage a third time, paying attention to the words and phrases that rest in your heart. What is God speaking to you through this passage?

2. Have you experienced suffering that seemed senseless to you?
3. Have the hardships you experienced drawn you closer to God or further away from him?
4. Would you be willing to invite Jesus into those dark areas of your suffering?

Mobilizing the Mission

In the next week, choose one of the following ways to be present to those that are suffering.

- Bring a meal to someone who is sick.
- Offer a Mass for a friend.
- Offer a Holy Hour for someone who is suffering.
- Pray the Divine Mercy for the terminally ill.
- Visit someone who has no one to visit him.

Closing Prayer

Heavenly Father, through the suffering of your Son and my savior, Jesus, I ask you to meet me in the shadowed moments of my own suffering. Please be with me in these memories and touch every tormented place in my heart. Speak to me about your saving love amid my heartache and allow me to rest in the assurance of your goodness even in this fallen world. Stay close and give me strength, comforting my aching heart. With your presence, reveal the light of your love and mercy through me. By the power of your redeeming love, repair what is broken and grant me the grace to be present, patient, and prayerful with others as they suffer.

Deacon Tom Thiltgen was ordained in 2001 and serves at Corpus Christi Parish in Carol Stream, IL. He currently works as a chaplain at Northwestern Medicine, Central DuPage Hospital. Deacon Tom is widowed and the father of three children and the grandfather of six grandsons. Deacon Tom grew up on a farm in Iowa and is a veteran of the US Army and worked as a marketing and sales professional in the corporate world for over thirty years prior to beginning full-time ministry.

CHAPTER 13

Terror of Demons

*"Joseph becomes the man of Divine election: the
man entrusted with a special responsibility."*[1]

—Pope St. John Paul II

How does the gentle St. Joseph earn the intriguing (and
sometimes exaggerated) title of Terror of Demons?
St. Joseph *is* the Terror of Demons because virtue terrifies
demons. Virtue, "the habitual and firm disposition to do
good,"[2] operates against the malicious rebellion of demonic
hate. This man, this saint, whom Holy Mother Church
unwaveringly calls "*most* just, *most* chaste, *most* prudent,
most strong, *most* obedient and *most* faithful," inhabits, by
grace, the attributes of Holy God. To the disobedient creature, one who perfectly does what God commands is a *holy*
terror.

As head of the Holy Family, St. Joseph's mission is one of
patrimony. He is the last patriarch, a "father over a family,"

---

[1]   Pope John Paul II, General Audience, March 19, 1980.
[2]   *Catechism of the Catholic Church* 1833.

of the Old Testament. He closes the work of the previous covenants as Jesus comes into the world to be the new and eternal covenant. Although St. Joseph does not generate his son, he receives him as so according to God's will. St. Joseph is the antithesis of King Herod, who kills his own sons to strengthen his hold on power. This saint's power comes through reception and custody, not in domination and fratricide. St. Joseph is a terror because he defends and protects Jesus's life and the virginal womb that bears and protects that life.

Finally, St. Joseph is a terror because he is wholly devoted to the care of the Blessed Mother of God. He takes her into his household and assumes the custodial care of her person. As directed by God, he defends this motherhood and, consequently, the life of Jesus. This faithful and loving devotion to endure all things for the care of Holy Mary and Jesus the Son is a terrible work against demons.

As you read Father Brady's story, pay attention to what stirs in your heart. Where are you living in the Father's will in your vocation and thus crushing the power of the devil? Where are you straying and giving him more power? Ask the Holy Spirit to gently show you your particular mission directed by the Father's holy will.

Wage War on Sin

Father Justin Brady

My relationship with St. Joseph started at birth. By the providence of God, I entered this world on March 19, the feast of St. Joseph. I have come to learn that these connections are tied into God's great economy of grace. God, who is omnipotent and omniscient, can inspire and direct these very encounters for his purpose. In my life, God did just that with St. Joseph.

My personal relationship with St. Joseph grew over time. My early understanding of him was filled with error and ignorance. At best, I saw him as an old fuddy-duddy who somehow guided the Blessed Mother of God and Jesus, her Son, to and fro. My understanding reflected the modernist distortion of St. Joseph as an un-virile, old chap, with the unspoken and incorrect narrative, "If he was young, you know, there is no way he could have loved Holy Mary in purity. Therefore, he was an old man beyond all those impulses." I do not know if this was my own error or one that I picked up from ill-formed Catholics, but the very idea is an accusation against the very virtues the Church professes in her Litany of St. Joseph.

Early in my life, I could not truly understand St. Joseph because I did not truly understand virtue. Like so many who are formed by distorted, secular thought, I could not yet grasp that the virtuous person does not deny passion but rather directs it to its proper end. That is, by grace, the passion remains undistorted, enabling one to live in freedom and not as a stoic. A virtuous person chooses to direct their interior and exterior life toward the good. As I matured in my knowledge of the Faith, I could see St. Joseph in the light of truth.

Thankfully, my simplistic view of St. Joseph matured with me. As a student at St. Joseph Catholic School, I loved the big statue of our patron in the chapel. I was drawn to its nobility and strength. However, it was not until my approaching ordination to the priesthood that my devotion deepened. As the time neared for me to become a spiritual father, I experienced a strong conviction to place myself under a saintly patron. While looking at various candidates, I was continuously drawn back to St. Joseph. Although I had some particular reasons, the experience was something supernatural. I was strongly compelled by spiritual intuition to place myself under his patronage. The spiritual economy of this act is still revealing itself to this day.

In the final years of my seminary formation, the scope of what God was inviting me into was becoming clearer, especially as God went about ordering my heart and strengthening my freedom to seek Holy Orders. I knew to be a priest meant I was to take a spouse and that one takes a spouse in order to become a father. A priest takes the Bride of Christ, the Church, as his spouse, and her children born from the womb of the baptismal font become his adopted spiritual sons and daughters.

I desired to be a genuine spiritual father. Therefore, I needed the assistance of a saint who understood this intimately. St. Joseph modeled how grace makes all things possible in this great call of discipleship. I wanted to be a man who defends Truth, Beauty, and Goodness, and I needed a patron who had been there and done that. Even better than that, one who is still on the very mission Holy God assigned to him so long ago.

St. Joseph was the custodian of the two greatest treasures creation will ever know: Mary, the Mother of God, and Jesus Christ the Lord. Pope St. John Paul II stated that St. Joseph

is "he to whom God entrusted the custody of His most precious treasures."[3] God trusted him in this role. God assigned
him this role. St. Joseph, "a just man" (Mt 1:19), responded
to God's will with the virtues fortified throughout his life.
As a priest, I desired to follow Joseph's example. My formation in seminary, in the early 2000s, was shadowed by the
wounds of priestly infidelity that became painfully public.
This scandal stirred in me an ardent desire to heal the body
of Christ. I never wanted to stain the Church and the holy
priesthood. I desired to help restore the image of fatherhood.
This fatherly zeal was reflected in my ordination holy card. It
bore an icon written by Brother Claude Lane, OSB, a monk
of Mont Angel Abbey in Oregon. The image is of St. Joseph
holding a child, face to his breast, living his role as our spiritual stepfather. The inscription I wrote below it read, "St.
Joseph, pray for me that I may love all with a father's heart."

I delight in God's holy economy, which placed St. Joseph
as my patron. This was not by merit but by God's will. It
speaks to the audacity of divine grace. It is the same reality
for me or any priest. As I celebrate and confer the holy sacraments, it brings me joy to know that it is God's will that
places me there. All I can do is offer my small *fiat* to his will,
which is easier in principle than in practice. I suspect, like
most parents, there is a tension between what I have to offer
and what I lack. St. Joseph reminds me to be less concerned
with my competency or merit and more aware of aligning
my will with the greater mission of God.

Mother Olga Yacob, the Mother Servant of Daughters of

---

[3]   Pope John Paul II, *Redemptoris Custos*, Apostolic Exhortation, Au-
        gust 15, 1989, no. 32.

Mary of Nazareth, illuminated for me a profound connection priests have with St. Joseph. Mother Olga, a self-professed adoptee of Holy Mary and Joseph, shared with delight as she held my hands how the priest at the consecration is the first to hold Jesus, the Word Become Flesh. Like holy St. Joseph at the Nativity, who first received Jesus in his hands and presented him to Mary, I, too, hold the adorable Jesus in my human hands. This transcendent reality became yet another reason to seek St. Joseph's patronage in my life.

I wish I had adequate words to describe the moment after consecration when I say, "Behold the Lamb of God." All I can say is that when I hold the Most Holy Eucharist, I am intensely aware that Jesus is a gift—a gift to be given to others. He is a treasure to be served and defended, and to be given and received. The depth of God's fatherly love for us continuously overwhelms me. I sense that St. Joseph was most acutely aware of this mystery as he first held God's fulfilled promise in his protective hands.

St. Joseph is wholly devoted to following the will of the Father. He faithfully reflects this by loving our Lady and our Lord as a spouse and father. As a priest, my obedience to the Father is to emulate Joseph. My daily life is to be directed to the mission of Jesus Christ and the honor of Holy Mary. I must go where God leads, like St. Joseph himself, who was instructed by angels in his mission. St. Joseph models what discipleship looks like in practice. One simply goes where he is instructed to go. St. Joseph is a "terror" because his response to the Father is *serviam*—that is, "I will serve". He submits to the Father's will as it is revealed to him. The response that precipitated the fall of the demons was their response of *non serviam*. St. Joseph, through his obedience, offers his own *fiat* to the Blessed Mother's (see Lk 1:38) and Jesus's (see Lk 22:42; Mk 14:36). Obedience and submission to the Father's will is a terror to demons.

In my spiritual life, I seek to always be conscious of my godly identity. What is this exactly? I am a beloved son of the Father, a man and a priest in Jesus Christ, a temple of the Holy Spirit, and a son of the Blessed Virgin Mary. This also means I am a son of St. Joseph and, by extension, a brother or godchild of all the saints. St. Joseph was a common man with uncommon virtue, a layman, and a worker who knew he was a son of God. This is my call too.

St. Joseph directs me to trust God's will and providence in my life. Why should I doubt my weakness when God chooses weakness as a constitutive component of his work? Often, I forget that what I perceive as personal strength in the lives of others, or in the saints, is really God's grace manifest through the virtues. If we were all a bit more like St. Joseph, we would spend less time listening to the enemy's lies about what we are not and more time living as the beloved sons and daughters we truly are.

In addition to my duties as a parish pastor, God, through the action of my bishop, has assigned me to the ministry of holy exorcism. It is important to remember this is an ordinary mission of Holy Mother Church, even if it may involve supernatural encounters. In the context of this ministry, the invocation, intercession, and veneration of St. Joseph is a terror to the fallen angels. *I have seen it firsthand.* St. Joseph is a powerful foe to the demonic. I have witnessed demons give testimony of his virtue, the authority of his intercession, and the humiliations they receive at his hands. It is important to understand that as a creature, an angel is a messenger of God. All angels were created to do God's will as directed, proper to their nature, mission, and personality. Demons seek to be what they are not. They serve only themselves. St. Joseph is a powerful intercessor against demons because he responds to God as he is: son, spouse, and father. He punishes them through his faithful acceptance of his purpose and mission. He moves with holy God, not against him.

It is here that St. Joseph is a model for all of us regardless of our state of life, gender, or vocation. When we respond to God as we are in him, we, too, can be a terror to demons. Like St. Joseph, only you can complete your unique mission. God's grace is sufficient for the call. The obedience, chastity, purity, humility, and fortitude of St. Joseph strengthens Holy Mother Church and her sons and daughters. He is the patron against all who would seek to bring her death and destruction. This was his mission for the Blessed Mother of God and Jesus Christ, the Incarnate Lord. This is his mission for you as well. That itself is a beautiful consolation.

St. Joseph, Terror of Demons, *pray for us!*

Engaging the Message

1. Pray with the following passage from Ephesians 6:12.

    "For we are not contending against flesh and blood, but against the principalities, against the powers, against the world rulers of this present darkness, against the spiritual hosts of wickedness in the heavenly places."

    •   Read the Scripture passage once and become familiar with the text.

- Slowly read the passage a second time.
- Very, very slowly read the passage a third time, paying attention to the words and phrases that rest in your heart. What is God speaking to you through this passage?

2. In what areas of your life are you submitting to the will of the Father and thus resisting the devil's schemes?
3. What areas of your life are you giving the devil access by running away from your God-given mission?
4. Are you willing to be led like St. Joseph?

Mobilizing the Mission

Look for opportunities every day to be a terror to demons by loving and serving God and your neighbor with virtue in your respective state and vocation. *Man your post.*

Closing Prayer

Heavenly Father, thank you for your unfailing love and protection. Please forgive me for the times that I have walked outside of your will and chosen my own path. Grant me the courage to serve like St. Joseph, to abide so fully in your will that my very footsteps instill terror in demons through his holy example of virtue, dependence, fatherhood, and service. Through your audacious grace, help me begin to fulfill this holy mission.

––––––––––

Reverend Justin Brady is a priest of the Diocese of Boise in Idaho. Ordained in 2005, he has been serving as a parish priest for sixteen years and within the Office of Healing,

Deliverance, and Exorcism for the past five years. A native Idahoan, and a son of the Mountain West, when not working, he will be found in the mountains and valleys of Idaho bicycling, skiing, and fly fishing.

Acknowledgments

We are deeply humbled by the Catholic leaders that contributed to this project. Your courageous stories and timeless wisdom will mobilize this critical mission.

For the unending encouragement and sacrifices of our family, we dedicate this book, especially our children: Anna, Drew, Ryan, Jack, Luke, Lily, Elle and Will. You are our core mission and most profound lifework. It is a privilege to be your parents.

We are also indebted to Dr. Bob Schuchts (Carrie's dad) and the entire staff at the John Paul II Healing Center for our collective vision of "Transformation in the Heart of the Church."

In deep gratitude to our Sacred Heart group specifically our fellow writing friends, Ann Salancy, Maria Buerkle and Danielle Chodorowski. Your contributions and insights over the years have been a cherished gift.

Finally, to Brian Kennelly and the team at TAN. It has been a joy to work with all of you. Thank you for believing in this mission..

Spiritual Warfare Prayers

Composed by Father Justin Brady

Prayer of Authority

O Most Holy Trinity, under you sovereign care, and in the authority of my holy baptism, I bind, sever, and cast out all demonic influence from _____ (my body, my spouse, my child, my possessions) and command it never to return. I pray you, O Lord, to expedite its exit and block its return. Fill me with grace that I, in your most faithful love, may be perfected in holy faith and fortitude. Holy God, I trust in you!

Prayer Invoking the Most Precious Blood

Lord Jesus Christ, by the power and grace of your Most Precious Blood, mercifully poured out for me from your Sacred Pierced Heart, deliver me from all demonic curses, hexes, and vexes, snares, knots, and entanglements. Be my defense and liberation against all who seek my harm. By your Most Precious Blood deliver me, O Lord, and bring blessing to all who wish ill to me, that they may turn to you, and know the joy of salvation. Amen.

Prayer to Saint Joseph

My Dearest Father, Most Holy Saint Joseph, I place myself under your mission and care. As you were assigned by God to defend our Infant Lord Jesus and the Most Blessed Mother, direct me as well along the paths of God's providential care. May you be my spiritual defense and a source of holy consolation amidst life's trials. Secure for me, by your intercession, faith, obedience, purity, and zealous love for Christ and Mary. O Saint Joseph, defend me now and direct me on the path to a holy life and death. Amen.

St. Joseph Novena

Oh, St. Joseph, whose protection is so great, so prompt, so strong, before the throne of God, I place in you all my interests and desires.

Oh, St. Joseph, do assist me by your powerful intercession, and obtain for me from your Divine Son all spiritual blessings, through Jesus Christ, our Lord. So that, having engaged here below your heavenly power, I may offer my thanksgiving and homage to the most Loving of Fathers.

Oh, St. Joseph, I never weary contemplating you and Jesus asleep in your arms; I dare not approach while He reposes near your heart. Press Him in my name and kiss His fine Head for me and Ask Him to return the Kiss when I draw my dying breath. St. Joseph, patron of departed souls, pray for me. Amen.

The Seven Privileges of St. Joseph

In *The Mystical City of God*, Venerable Abbess Maria de Jesus de Ágreda, the seventeenth-century Spanish Franciscan mystic, wrote of "certain privileges in favor of those who choose [St. Joseph] for their intercessor, and who invoke him with devotion." Maria lists these as:

1. Obtain the virtue of chastity and be withdrawn from the danger of losing it.
2. Receive powerful assistance to be freed from sin and to recover the grace of God.
3. Acquire, by his means, devotion for the Blessed Lady, and dispositions to receive her favors.
4. Receive the grace of a happy death and special protection against demons at this last hour.
5. To intimidate enemies of our salvation by pronouncing the name of St. Joseph.
6. Obtain health of body and consolation in affliction.
7. To have successors in families.

About the Authors

Duane and Carrie established Team Daunt in 1999 when they were married in the Church. They are the parents of eight energetic children and reside in Tallahassee, Florida. Duane and Carrie both work for the John Paul II Healing Center. In addition to his work in business development for a large software company, Duane is a business consultant for the Center. Carrie is a content developer and presenter for the Center's *Undone* women's conferences, a prayer minister for the *Healing the Whole Person* events, and a co-presenter for the *Unveiled* marriage conference. Carrie is also author of *Undone: Freeing Your Feminine Heart from the Knots of Fear and Shame*. Together they enjoy spending time with family and watching their kids play soccer. They have been involved in marriage ministry and presented locally and nationally at different events and conferences over the last twenty-one years. With a devotion to the Holy Family, they are thrilled to launch the *Man Your Post* mission to help restore masculinity through the holy example of St. Joseph.